Wisdom of Bhagavad Gītā

through

Tales of Mahābhārata

Science + values

Lajjāvatī Devī Dāsī

Copyright © 2005 Lakshmi Patel

All Rights Reserved.

This book has been self-published with all reasonable efforts taken to make the material error-free by the author. No part of this book shall be used, reproduced in any manner whatsoever without written permission from the author, except in the case of brief quotations embodied in critical articles and reviews.

The Author of this book is solely responsible and liable for its content including but not limited to the views, representations, descriptions, statements, information, opinions and references ["Content"]. The Content of this book shall not constitute or be construed or deemed to reflect the opinion or expression of the Publisher or Editor. Neither the Publisher nor Editor endorse or approve the Content of this book or guarantee the reliability, accuracy or completeness of the Content published herein and do not make any representations or warranties of any kind, express or implied, including but not limited to the implied warranties of merchantability, fitness for a particular purpose. The Publisher and Editor shall not be liable whatsoever for any errors, omissions, whether such errors or omissions result from negligence, accident, or any other cause or claims for loss or damages of any kind, including without limitation, indirect or consequential loss or damage arising out of use, inability to use, or about the reliability, accuracy or sufficiency of the information contained in this book.

Made with ❤ on the Notion Press Platform

www.notionpress.com

Contents

CONTENTS

1. Introduction

The Mahābhārata, one of the greatest epics of ancient India, is a treasure trove of wisdom, values, and timeless lessons. Its creation is as extraordinary as its content. Sage Vyāsadeva, inspired to compose this monumental work, sought the help of Lord Gaṇeśa to transcribe it. Gaṇeśa agreed, but with a condition: Vyāsa must recite the epic without pause. Vyāsadeva agreed but cleverly added his own condition: Gaṇeśa must fully understand each verse before writing it. Thus, the collaboration of divine intellect and unwavering focus gave birth to this epic.

Spanning 18 chapters and over 100,000 verses, the Mahābhārata is the longest epic in the world describing the activities of the Kuru dynasty, weaving together profound philosophical teachings, riveting narratives, and invaluable life lessons.

The Bhagavad Gītā is a pivotal section of the Mahābhārata, nestled within the Bhīṣma Parva (Book of Bhīṣma). It unfolds on the battlefield of Kurukṣetra as a dialogue between Lord Śrī Kṛṣṇa and Arjuna, just before the great war begins. Faced with a moral crisis, Arjuna hesitates to fight, overwhelmed by doubts and familial attachments. In response, Kṛṣṇa imparts timeless spiritual wisdom, addressing the nature of dharma, ātmā, and the ultimate purpose of life.

The Mahābhārata is thus, not merely a story but a guide to living a righteous and meaningful life, encompassing themes like duty, relationships, morality, and the eternal battle between good and evil. `

For young readers, the Mahābhārata holds immense significance. It provides relatable examples of how to navigate the challenges of life, the importance of standing by dharma (righteousness), and the consequences of choices driven by jealousy, pride, or selfishness. These lessons are especially relevant for young people, as they begin to make decisions that shape their future.

This book brings to life some of the most well-known and powerful episodes from the Mahābhārata, presented in a way that is both engaging and meaningful for young readers. Each chapter explores key moments from the epic, drawing out timeless values and life lessons. These stories offer a practical framework for developing important qualities like respect, patience, courage, and self-discipline, while also helping readers recognize the dangers of envy, pride, and greed.

Beyond simply teaching values, the book shows how these lessons connect deeply with the path of Kṛṣṇa-bhakti. Each insight is framed to help young minds understand how cultivating these virtues nourishes devotion and brings them closer to Lord Kṛṣṇa.

Importantly, the teachings of the Bhagavad Gītā are not only timeless but also remarkably relevant to modern science and psychology. Where appropriate, this book draws parallels between the Gītā's insights and contemporary scientific findings. For example, verse 18.37, which speaks of long-term happiness arising from initial difficulty, can be linked to the famous Stanford Marshmallow Experiment, which demonstrated the value of self-control and delayed gratification. In this way, the wisdom of the Gītā resonates with even the most modern understandings of the human mind and behaviour.

To the young readers: as you journey through this book, reflect deeply on the lessons learned. Look at the situations in your life, the challenges you face, and the decisions you must make. Apply the values and teachings from the Mahābhārata to grow into individuals who are wise, compassionate, and resolute in upholding dharma. Let this epic not only inspire you but also shape your character as you step into the world.

As you delve into the Mahābhārata, you'll notice that the values and societal norms of its time often differ significantly from those of the modern world. For instance, practices such as the svayamvara, where a princess chose her husband through a contest, reflect the customs and traditions of that era.

It's important to approach these stories with an open mind, understanding that the Mahābhārata reflects the cultural, moral, and social context of its era. These narratives provide valuable insights into timeless human emotions, relationships, and dilemmas, even if the specific customs or actions seem distant from our current experiences.

Embrace these differences as an opportunity to learn and reflect on how values evolve over time while still resonating with universal principles like duty, love, and compassion.

In this book, Sanskrit words have been presented with diacritics to ensure their pronunciation and transliteration are accurately represented, adhering to the IAST (International Alphabet of Sanskrit Transliteration) system. **Appendix 4** on pronunciation has been provided to assist readers unfamiliar with these notations.

2. Dharma – the central theme of the Mahābhārata

Dharma, the principle of righteousness and duty, is the central theme of the Mahābhārata, weaving through its complex narrative and guiding the actions of its characters. It is portrayed not as a fixed code but as a dynamic concept, requiring discernment and wisdom to navigate.

The epic explores the conflicts and challenges of adhering to dharma, especially when moral duties clash, such as in Arjuna's reluctance to fight in the war and Yudhiṣṭhira's dilemma over truth and duty. Through its multifaceted stories, the Mahābhārata teaches that dharma is the foundation of personal conduct and social harmony, urging individuals to reflect deeply on their responsibilities and choices.

What is dharma?

The word dharma has no direct translation into English. It comes from the Sanskrit root dhṛ, which means to uphold, sustain, or uplift. Dharma is the innate characteristic that makes something what it is. It is the pursuit and execution of one's nature and true calling. For example, it is the dharma of the bee to make honey, of the cow to give milk, of the sun to radiate sunshine, and of the river to flow.

The Śrīmad Bhāgavata says that dharma is that which is taught by Bhagavān through his words and deeds1.

In terms of humanity, dharma is the need for, the effect of and essence of service and interconnectedness of all life. It can be thought of as righteousness in thought, word, and action. It is the thing that regulates the course of change by not participating in that change, but that principle which remains constant. Thus, dharma is defined as "dhārayati iti dharmaḥ" - the collection of natural and universal laws that uphold, sustain, or uplift. These laws include the law of one's being (one's innate nature), law of nature, prescribed duties, social and personal duties, moral codes, civil laws, codes of conduct, morality, way of life, practice, justice, righteousness, religion, harmony and so on. Each of these laws is incomplete in itself as a definition, while the combination of these does not convey the total sense of the word. In common parlance, dharma means "right way of living" and "path of rightness". The meaning of the word dharma therefore depends on the context.

Aspects of dharma

Some of the aspects of dharma include:

- sanātana dharma – the eternal and unchanging principals of dharma.

- vyakti dharma / svadharma – the duties of an individual

- varṇāśramā dharma – one's duty at specific stages of life or inherent duties.

- āpad dharma – dharma prescribed at the time of adversities.

- sādhārana dharma – moral duties irrespective of the stages of life.

- samāja dharma – duties towards the society one lives in.

- rāṣṭra dharma – duties towards one's nation.

- yuga dharma – dharma which is valid for a yuga, an epoch or age. The yuga dharma for the current yuga, Kaliyuga, is chanting the Lord's names.

- bhagavad dharma – duties centred on spiritual love and devotion for Kṛṣṇa and leading eternal service to Kṛṣṇa in the spiritual world, as taught in the Śrīmad Bhāgavata Purāṇa. These include the study of scriptures, following the processes of bhakti like śravaṇam, kīrtanam, smaraṇam and so on, service (sevā) to the deity and devotees of the Lord, and leading a moral and ethical life.

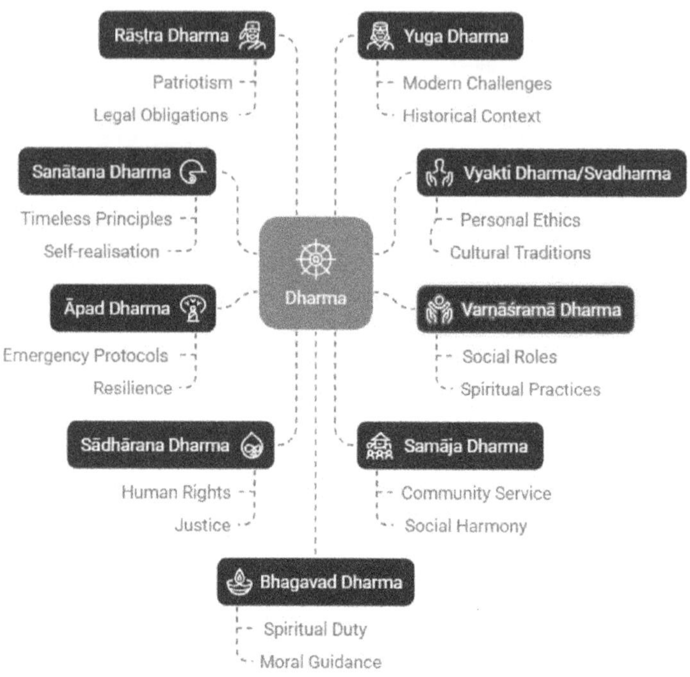

Dharma in the Bhagavad Gītā 1.1

The very first word of the Bhagavad Gītā is "dharma". The first verse is:

dhṛtarāṣṭra uvāca
dharma-kṣetre kuru-kṣetre samavetā yuyutsavaḥ
māmakāḥ pāṇḍavāś caiva kim akurvata sañjaya

Dhṛtarāṣṭra said: O Sañjaya, my sons and the sons of Pāṇḍu who were assembled in the field of dharma, Kurukṣetra, desiring to fight, what did they do?

Here, Dhṛtarāṣṭra refers to Kurukṣetra as a dharma-kṣetra, the "field of dharma." This reference highlights the battlefield not only as a physical location but also as a symbolic ground for testing dharma – righteousness, duty, and moral principles.

Dhṛtarāṣṭra's question to Sañjaya reveals his anxiety about the outcome, reflecting his internal conflict: he knows that his sons have deviated from dharma, yet his attachment blinds him. His query foreshadows the complex dilemmas faced by every character, especially Arjuna, who is paralyzed by doubt about his own dharma as a warrior.

Thus, the Bhagavad Gītā verse 1.1 connects deeply to the Mahābhārata's broader narrative, initiating a discussion on dharma that Kṛṣṇa resolves through His teachings, guiding Arjuna – and humanity – toward understanding true dharma as devotion and surrender to the Supreme.

In the Bhagavad Gītā verse 4.7, Śrī Kṛṣṇa says that he descends to this world to establish dharma and eliminate evil, thus restoring balance:

yadā yadā hi dharmasya glānir bhavati bhārata abhyutthānam adharmasya tadātmānaṁ sṛjāmy aham

Verse 4.8 highlights three purposes of Kṛṣṇa's incarnation: to protect the righteous (sādhūnām); to annihilate the wicked (duṣkṛtām), and, to reestablish dharma (righteousness):

paritrāṇāya sādhūnām vināśāya ca duṣkṛtām dharma-saṁsthāpanārthāya sambhavāmi yuge yuge

Dharma in context

Dharma thus represents the eternal cosmic law and individual duties aligned with one's role in society and spiritual life. Over time, adharma (unrighteousness) often overtakes dharma due to greed, corruption, and neglect of moral principles. Śrī Kṛṣṇa's descent occurs at such critical junctures when humanity needs divine intervention to restore balance.

In the Mahābhārata, Kṛṣṇa actively ensures the triumph of dharma through His guidance of the Pāṇḍavas. His teachings to Arjuna in the Bhagavad Gītā provide clarity on svadharma (one's duty) and transcendental dharma, emphasizing the importance of acting without attachment, solely as service to the Supreme.

Therefore, dharma can be followed simply by following the teachings of Śrī Kṛṣṇa. The Mahābhārata supports this by stating repeatedly with slight variations - where there is dharma there is Kṛṣṇa, and where there is Kṛṣṇa there is victory[2].

The Mahābhārata also avers that those who uphold and protect dharma (righteousness or duty) will themselves be protected by it. This principle is translated into practice by various scriptures like the Mahābhārata and Manu Smṛti that exhort the practice of dharma through the statement dharmo rakṣati rakṣitaḥ. This translates to "dharma protects those who protect it." The statement essentially means that those who uphold and protect dharma (righteousness or duty) will themselves be protected by it. Conversely, those who violate dharma will face destruction.

In the Mahābhārata, dharma is a central theme, governing the decisions and conflicts of the epic. The Pandavas and Kauravas, though related, embody conflicting approaches to dharma. Kurukṣetra becomes the ultimate proving ground where the

---

[2] There are numerous variations of this statement spoken by various persons in the Mahābhārata. E.g., *yato dharmastataḥ kṛṣṇo yataḥ kṛṣṇastato jayaḥ* | (Mahabharata 6.23.28, 6.43.60 and 9.62.31); *yataḥ kṛṣṇastato dharmo yato dharmastato jayaḥ* | (Mahabharata 6.66.35 and 13.167.41)

consequences of adharma (unrighteousness) and adherence to dharma unfold.

Dharma in Kṛṣṇa-bhakti

In bhakti, dharma is understood as "sanātana-dharma", the eternal duty of the jīva, which is pure devotional service (bhakti) to Kṛṣṇa. Unlike the material concept of svadharma (duties based on one's svabhāva (nature), role, or societal position), the highest dharma is bhagavata-dharma, or unalloyed surrender and service to the Supreme Lord.

The key aspects of dharma in Kṛṣṇa-bhakti include:

- Sanātana-dharma (eternal duty): The jīva's true identity is as an eternal servant (nitya-dāsa) of Kṛṣṇa. Bhakti is the highest dharma: Loving devotional service (prema-bhakti) is the ultimate duty, beyond Vedic rituals and societal roles.

- Rejecting material dharma when it conflicts with bhakti: If varna-āśrama dharma (social duty) hinders devotion, a devotee prioritizes direct engagement in Kṛṣṇa's service. This is demonstrated in the Bhagavad Gītā when initially Arjuna faces a dharma-saṅkaṭa (crisis of duty), where his kṣatriya-dharma (warrior duty) clashes with his compassion for family members. There is however a transition from kṣatriya-dharma to bhagavata-dharma as Kṛṣṇa later instructs Arjuna to abandon all varieties of dharma and surrender unto him alone. (BG 18.663) This

---

[3] *sarva-dharmān parityajya mām ekaṁ śaraṇaṁ vraja*
ahaṁ tvāṁ sarva-pāpebhyo mokṣayiṣyāmi mā śucaḥ
Abandon all dharma and just surrender unto Me. I shall deliver you from all sinful reactions. Do not fear. (BG 18.66)

does not mean that Arjuna should abandon his duty as a warrior and refuse to fight. Instead, it means he should perform his duty with complete dependence on Kṛṣṇa and without material attachment. True surrender does not mean inaction; it means acting according to Kṛṣṇa's will, without selfish motives.

3. The epic begins

The story of Mahābhārata traces its roots to King Duśyanta, a mighty ruler of ancient India. Duṣyanta married Śakuntalā, the foster-daughter of the sage Kaṇva. Śakuntalā was born to Menakā, an apsarā4 of Indra's court, and the sage Viśvāmitra.

Śakuntalā and Duṣyanta's son, Bharata, grew to be a great warrior. Bharata is credited with uniting vast territories across the Indian subcontinent, giving rise to the term "Bhārata-varṣa," which is used to refer to India even today. Bharata's kingdom was a vast empire encompassing numerous regions and principalities, far beyond the boundaries of what later became the Kuru kingdom with Hastināpura as its capital. In contrast, Hastināpura, though significant, was primarily the heart of the Kuru dynasty and represented a smaller, albeit powerful, region within Bhārata-varṣa.

The Mahābhārata, meaning "the story of the descendants of Bharata," begins with King Śāntanu, a noble and wise ruler of Hastināpura. One day, while hunting, Śāntanu ventured into a forest and reached the banks of the Ganges. There, he was mesmerized by the sight of a beautiful woman walking on the river's surface. This was no ordinary woman; she was a divine being, and Śāntanu was struck by her grace.

"Who are you?" asked Śāntanu, his voice filled with awe. "I am captivated by your beauty. I, Śāntanu, king of Hastināpura, wish to marry you."

---

[4] A class of female divinities or celestial damsels who reside in the sky and are regarded as the wives of the Gandharvas.

The woman, who was Gaṅgādevī, responded with a condition. "I will marry you, but you must swear to never question me about my past or my actions. And you must never stop me from doing anything, no matter what."

Śāntanu, overwhelmed by her charm, agreed to her terms, and they were married.

Years passed, and Gaṅgā gave birth to a son. But to Śāntanu's horror, the queen took the newborn and left him in the river Gaṅgā. Shocked and heartbroken, Śāntanu could not stop her, bound by the promise he had made. This occurred each time Gaṅgā gave birth – she would leave the child in the river. Seven sons perished this way.

Finally, when the eighth son was born, Śāntanu could bear no more. As Gaṅgā took the child toward the river, Śāntanu cried out, "Stop! I cannot stand to lose another son! Please, stop!"

Gaṅgā turned, her face full of sadness. "You have broken your word, O King. But before I leave you, I will reveal the truth. Your sons were not ordinary children. They were the divine Vasus, cursed to be born on Earth as humans because of a past misdeed. Seven of them would die and return to heaven immediately after birth. The eighth, however, would live out his life here on Earth, and I, as part of my mission, was to raise him."

With those words, Gaṅgā took the child and disappeared.

Years later, King Śāntanu was walking by the river when Gaṅgā appeared once more, holding the now grown-up boy. "Here is your son, Deva-vrata," Gaṅgā said. "He is strong and ready for his destiny."

Śāntanu was overjoyed and declared Deva-vrata as his heir. Deva-vrata was an ideal heir a brave warrior and of noble character.

As the years passed, King Śāntanu grew older and lonely. One day, while walking by the river again, he met another woman, Satyavatī, the daughter of a fisherman. She had a special fragrance, and Śāntanu was immediately enchanted by her.

Unbeknownst to him, Satyavatī had a secret. In her youth, she had been blessed by the sage Parāśara, who gave her a divine fragrance and a boon to have a son. That son was Vyāsa, the sage who would later compose the Mahābhārata.

Śāntanu, unaware of Satyavatī's past, approached her father to ask for her hand. The fisherman agreed, but on one condition – any son born to Satyavatī would inherit the throne of Hastināpura, not Deva-vrata. Devastated, Śāntanu returned to his palace.

But Deva-vrata, upon finding out the reason for his father's unhappiness, went to Satyavatī's father and said, "I promise that I hereby renounce my claim to the throne of Hastināpura. Any son born to my father and Satyavatī will become the king." The fisherman, still uncertain, asked, "But what about your children? They could challenge the throne."

In the act of supreme sacrifice, Deva-vrata said, "I vow to remain celibate for life, never to marry. I shall devote myself to the service of the kingdom and its ruler." This vow earned him the name Bhīṣma, meaning "the one who took a terrible vow." Śāntanu, moved by his son's devotion, granted Bhīṣma a special boon – the ability to choose the time of his death.

Śāntanu and Satyavatī were married, and they had two sons, Citraṅgada and Vicitravīrya. After Śāntanu's death, Citraṅgada became king, but he was killed in battle. Vicitravīrya ascended the throne, but he died young without an heir.

Satyavatī, in desperation, called for her first son, Vyāsa. Vyāsa, at her request, blessed the widows of Vicitravīrya, Ambikā and Ambālikā, with sons. The eldest, Dhṛtarāṣṭra, was born blind, and the younger, Pāṇḍu, was pale and sickly. Vyāsa also blessed a maid of one of queens with a son, Vidura, the wise. He was made the chief advisor to the king.

Dhṛtarāṣṭra married Gāndhārī, who, in an act of love and loyalty, blindfolded herself forever.

Pāṇḍu married Kuntī and Mādrī. After a tragic accident in which Pāṇḍu killed a deer while it was mating, he was cursed to die if he ever touched his wives. Fearing for his life, Pāṇḍu and his wives left the palace and lived as hermits in the forest.

There, Kuntī revealed a secret – she had once been blessed by a sage with a mantra that allowed her to summon any deva to bear children. Using this mantra, Kuntī was blessed with

Yudhiṣṭhira, the eldest, who was born from Dharma, the god of righteousness; Bhīma from Vāyu, the god of wind; and Arjuna from Indra, the king of the gods. She taught the mantra to Mādrī who bore the twins, Nakula and Sahadeva, born from the Aśvinī twins.

To secure an heir, Gāndhārī prayed for a hundred sons. Vyāsa, with his powers, granted her wish. Duryodhana was born as the eldest, followed by his ninety-nine brothers and one sister.

Lessons to be learned

Sacrifice and devotion – Bhīṣma's vow to renounce his claim to the throne and remain celibate demonstrates selflessness and devotion to his father's happiness and the greater good.

Values reflected

Self-discipline (tapas) and Respect (ādara): For the wishes and well-being of others, even at great personal cost.

4. The poisoning of Bhīma

Soon thereafter, Pāṇḍu died and Kuntī and the five Pāṇḍavas returned to Hastināpura, the capital of the Kurus. The Pāṇḍavas were raised alongside their cousins, the Kauravas.

As a child, Bhīma's strength was always on display, much to Duryodhana's frustration.

"Bhīma wins every time!" Duryodhana grumbled after another game. His jealousy simmered until Duryodhana hatched a dark plan.

One day, he offered Bhīma a feast laced with poison. As Bhīma fell unconscious, Duryodhana ordered his men, "Throw him into the river."

But as Bhīma sank, he reached the underwater realm of the Nāgas, where serpents bit him, neutralizing the poison in his body. Revived, he met Āryaka, a grandfather of Kuntī, who was a Nāga chief. Āryaka introduced Bhīma to Vāsuki, the Nāga king.

Learning of his parentage, Vāsuki offered him an elixir. "Drink this, Bhīma, it will give you with the strength of a thousand elephants". Bhīma drank deeply. After eight days of rest, he returned to Hastināpura, more powerful than ever.

The Pāṇḍavas and Kuntī were overjoyed to see him. They had given him up for dead and had lost all hope. Hearing Bhīma's story, Kuntī was filled with immense concern. She called Vidura and confided in him, "Duryodhana is wicked and cruel. He seeks to kill Bhīma so he can seize the throne. I am deeply worried."

Vidura replied thoughtfully, "What you say is true, but keep these thoughts to yourself. If Duryodhana is accused or confronted, his anger and hatred will only intensify. Rest assured, your sons are blessed with long lives and are protected by the devas. You need not fear for their safety."

Yudhiṣṭhira, too, cautioned Bhīma. "Say nothing of this matter. From now on, we must remain vigilant, support one another, and ensure our own protection."

When Duryodhana saw Bhīma return unharmed, he was shocked. His jealousy and hatred only grew stronger, and he sank deeper into frustration and despair.

Lessons to be learned

- Strength comes from adversity – Challenges, even those born of malice, can be opportunities for growth. Bhīma's poisoning led to his encounter with the Nāgas and the boon of immense strength.

- Jealousy breeds harm – Duryodhana's envy drove him to commit a heinous act, highlighting the destructive nature of unchecked jealousy.

- Divine providence and resilience – Bhīma's survival and subsequent empowerment demonstrate that divine forces often protect those destined for greatness.

- Wisdom in handling adversity – Vidura advises caution and discretion when dealing with Duryodhana's malice. This highlights the importance of understanding human nature and acting prudently to prevent further harm.

- Unity and vigilance – Yudhiṣṭhira emphasizes the need for mutual support and vigilance among the brothers, demonstrating the strength of unity in facing challenges.

Values reflected

- Courage (dhairya): Bhīma's bravery and resilience in the face of danger, and the Pāṇḍavas' ability to remain calm and resolute in the face of danger reflects their inner strength and courage.

- Respect (ādara): Kuntī shows respect for Vidura's wisdom and seeks his guidance, reflecting the importance of valuing knowledgeable advisors.

- Wisdom (viveka): Vidura's counsel showcases the importance of careful thought and strategic silence to manage difficult situations.

- Patience (titikṣā): Kuntī and Yudhiṣṭhira exhibit patience by choosing restraint and preparation over confrontation.

- Self-discipline (tapas): Bhīma adheres to Yudhiṣṭhira's advice, demonstrating the discipline required to keep personal emotions in check for the greater good.

5. The training of the princes, Ekalavya, and the great competition

Pāṇḍu's sons, the Pāṇḍavas, and Dhṛtarāṣṭra's sons, the Kauravas, grew strong under the guidance of their teacher, Droṇācārya. There were many other students in the gurukula like Karṇa, and members of the Vṛṣṇis and Andhaka kingdoms. Droṇācārya was an expert in weaponry having learned from the most powerful Paraśurāma. He had taken a vow to break the pride of his old friend, King Drupada, who had wronged him. One day, Droṇa asked all his students, "Will you do me a favour when you are all proficient in using your weapons?" No one spoke except little Arjuna who said, "I promise, gurudeva." This made Arjuna Droṇa's favourite student. He therefore promised to make Arjuna the foremost archer in the world.

One day, a youth named Ekalavya approached Droṇācārya. Bowing respectfully, he said, "O revered teacher, I am Ekalavya, son of the king of the Niṣādas, Hiraṇyadhanu. Please accept me as your disciple and teach me the art of archery."

Droṇācārya knew that King Hiraṇyadhanu was a general in the army of Jarāsandha, a known adversary of the Kuru. He therefore said, "I cannot be your teacher, Ekalavya. Please find another guru."

Ekalavya said, "Guru Droṇa, even if you cannot formally accept me, I will always consider you my teacher." He then left the gurukula and going into the forest, crafted an image of Droṇācārya from clay. He practiced diligently day and night before the image, honing his skills with unwavering dedication. As a result of his exceptional reverence for his preceptor and his devotion to his purpose, he became an archer of extraordinary ability.

One day, Droṇācārya and the Kuru princes went for a hunting excursion into the forest. Their dog, wandering in the woods came upon Ekalavya whose body was besmeared with filth, dressed in black and bearing matted locks on head. Startled, the dog began to bark at him. Wishing to show off his skill with the bow, Ekalavya shot seven arrows into its mouth before the dog could shut it without even looking at it – simply by hearing the sound of the barking.

The princes were amazed by this mastery of shooting and approaching Ekalavya asked, "Who are you? Who is your teacher?"

Ekalavya introduced himself and pointed to the clay idol. "My guru is Droṇācārya. I have learned everything from him."

The princes went back and told Droṇācārya about Ekalavya and his skill. Arjuna turned to his guru and asked innocently, "Gurudeva, you had hugged me and told me that I would be the greatest archer. Why then is another student of yours greater than I am?"

Droṇācārya, taking Arjuna, went to see Ekalavya. After being respectfully worshipped by Ekalavya, he said, "If I am truly your guru, you must offer me a guru-dakṣiṇā, a teacher's fee."

Hearing these cruel words, Ekalavya replied without hesitation, "Anything you ask, I will gladly give."

Droṇācārya said, "Then I ask for your right thumb."

Ekalavya, unwavering in his respect, cheerfully took out his blade and severed his right thumb without a moment's hesitation, placing it at Droṇācārya's feet. He then went back to his practice, but he had lost his lightness of hand.

Arjuna decided to become the best archer in the world. He practised day and night and even in the dark. His entire focus was on mastering the bow and becoming exceptional. Soon he was unmatched in his skill and earned himself the title of "Jiṣṇu" meaning triumphant and always victorious. He could shoot arrows using both hands and this earned him the title of "Savyasācī". He could use mantras to control the elements like the wind, water and fire. He could cause the appearance of the Brahmāstra, the most powerful weapon, but more importantly, he could also withdraw the Brahmāstra.

Throughout the Mahābhārata, there are many examples of Arjuna's skill. He truly was the world's topmost archer.

Arjuna exemplifies the importance of staying focused on one's goal to achieve success. He employs the principle of delayed gratification, understanding that immediate pleasures must be set aside to attain greater, long-term achievements. However, Arjuna also realizes that mastering this technique requires managing the mind.

Two verses from the Bhagavad Gītā help us understand these concepts: 18.37 and 6.5.

Bhagavad Gītā 18.37

In Bhagavad Gītā 18.37, Śrī Kṛṣṇa says:

yat tad agre viṣam iva pariṇāme 'mṛtopamam
tat sukhaṁ sāttvikaṁ proktam ātma-buddhi-prasāda-jam

That which in the beginning may be just like poison but at the end is just like nectar and which awakens one to self-realization is said to be happiness in the mode of goodness.

BG 18.37 with respect to Ekalavya and Arjuna

Connection with Ekalavya

Ekalavya's perseverance and devotion embody the spirit of this verse. Although Droṇācārya rejected him as a formal disciple, Ekalavya faced this initial bitterness by pursuing self-discipline and practice. However, his joy was incomplete as his pursuit of mastery, though sincere, was detached from rightful guidance and therefore, from dharma.

Connection with Arjuna

Arjuna's commitment to archery, even practicing at night by candlelight, perfectly aligns with the sāttvika ideal. His initial efforts were arduous, requiring immense focus and self-discipline. Yet, these challenges ultimately bore fruit, as his mastery over archery was unparalleled, and it brought him the joy of fulfilling his dharma as a warrior. Arjuna's sāttvika happiness was grounded in dharma and proper guidance under Droṇācārya.

Message in the context of Kṛṣṇa-bhakti

The concept of sāttvika happiness aligns with the principle of enduring temporary hardships for eternal spiritual bliss. Devotional service (bhakti) may seem challenging at first – requiring self-restraint, humility, and surrender – but it ultimately leads to eternal happiness in Kṛṣṇa's service.

- Detachment from immediate gratification: Both Ekalavya's discipline and Arjuna's dedication reflect the detachment from comfort and ease, which bhakti advocates in pursuing higher spiritual goals.

- Proper guidance in bhakti: The success of one's spiritual and material endeavours is guaranteed when one acts under the proper guidance of a bona fide guru, as Arjuna does under Droṇa and later Śrī

Kṛṣṇa.

- Eternal bliss through bhakti: The verse reflects the bhakti view that sāttvika joy, while cultivated through discipline, ultimately yields the nectar of loving Kṛṣṇa, which surpasses all temporary struggles.

Thus, this verse, when seen through the lens of these Mahābhārata incidents, illustrates that challenges, discipline, and proper spiritual alignment lead to fulfilment both in one's duties and in the eternal bliss of devotional service.

BG 18.37 and modern psychology

This verse describes sāttvika happiness or the process of delayed gratification. The Stanford Marshmallow Experiment is a psychological study that tested delayed gratification in children. It demonstrated that those who could endure initial discomfort (waiting for a larger reward later rather than taking a smaller immediate reward) tended to achieve greater success in life.

For details about this experiment and how it can be applied to the lives of young people, see **Appendix 1**.

Bhagavad Gītā 6.5

In Bhagavad Gītā 6.5, Śrī Kṛṣṇa says:

uddhared ātmanātmānaṁ nātmānam avasādayet
ātmaiva hy ātmano bandhur ātmaiva ripur ātmanaḥ

One must deliver himself with the help of his mind and not degrade himself. The mind is one's friend, and his enemy as well.

BG 6.5 with respect to Arjuna

This principle is exemplified by Arjuna's dedication to practicing archery even in the dark of the night. Realizing his potential was limited by external factors (like daylight), Arjuna chose to take charge of his own progress. His unwavering focus and determination to overcome limitations represent the idea of uplifting oneself through conscious effort, as instructed in BG 6.5. Arjuna's mind, managed and disciplined, became his ally in achieving mastery of his craft.

Arjuna practiced a strict physical discipline, controlling his diet, exercise and sleep (earning the name Guḍākeṣa meaning one who has conquered sleep). He approached his studies with humility and attention, absorbing lessons about strategy, ethics, and higher values that a warrior needs. His mental discipline ensured he grew holistically with a sharp focus, and balanced emotions. Arjuna's ability to manage his emotions – like anger, frustration, or fear – was critical to his success. Instead of succumbing to negativity, he channelled his emotions into focused effort, thereby ensuring that his mind remained a friend. He transformed his mind into an ally rather than an obstacle, illustrating the principle of self-upliftment through conscious effort.

In the context of Kṛṣṇa-bhakti

The same principle of self-effort and discipline applies to one's spiritual practice (sādhanā). A devotee must take personal responsibility to uplift oneself through consistent bhakti (devotional service) and managing the vagaries of the mind. The mind can either be a friend, guiding one toward the lotus feet of Śrī Kṛṣṇa, or an enemy, distracting one with worldly desires. Just as Arjuna overcame challenges through focus, devotees are encouraged to persevere in their spiritual practices, such as chanting the holy names (nāma-japa), studying scriptures, and performing devotional service, regardless of difficulties. By doing so, they uplift themselves and draw closer to Kṛṣṇa, fulfilling the essence of BG 6.5.

To see how BG 6.5 can be applied to the lives of young people, see **Appendix 2**.

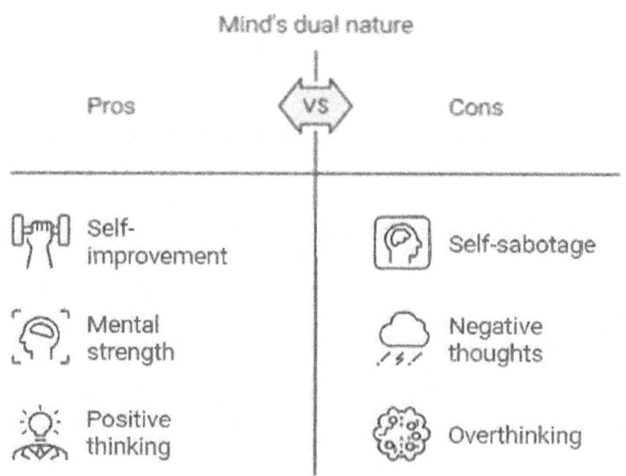

The royal princes had finished their rigorous training under Droṇācārya. The day had come for them to showcase their skills in a grand competition arranged by grandsire Bhīṣma. Dignitaries from all over the land gathered to witness the spectacle.

The competition began with the archery contest, and Arjuna, with his unmatched skill, drew everyone's attention. His arrows flew with incredible precision, hitting the target effortlessly. He impressed not only the royals but also the common people who had gathered to watch.

As the event neared its end, a figure suddenly appeared in the distance. It was Karṇa, a young warrior none of them had seen before, but his presence was commanding. Karṇa was a charioteer's son.

Karṇa stepped forward confidently. "I challenge Arjuna to a duel," he declared.

Kṛpācārya, another exalted teacher, frowned and spoke up. "This competition is meant only for the royal princes who have been invited to participate. Also, the arena here is specially constructed for the Kuru princes to demonstrate their skills before the people of Hastināpura. It is not to be used for a duel."

This argument infuriated Duryodhana, who was always envious of the Pāṇḍavas. To support Karṇa and counter Kṛpācārya's objection, Duryodhana declared, "This man, Karṇa, is no ordinary person. I will make him a prince," he said with determination." Turning to Karṇa, he said, "You shall rule over Aṅga, and as a prince, you will become worthy to compete."

However, by the time this argument, Duryodhana's intervention, and the anointment of Karṇa as the King of Aṅga concluded, the sun had set. According to the customs of that time, battles could not be conducted after sunset, so the duel was postponed and ultimately did not take place that day.

This incident set the stage for the lifelong rivalry between Karṇa and Arjuna and strengthened Karṇa's loyalty to Duryodhana, marking a pivotal moment in the epic.

Lessons to be learned

- Respect for dedication and commitment – Arjuna's unwavering dedication to his training, teaches the value of self-discipline and respect for the pursuit of excellence. His respect for his teacher, shown by practicing diligently, highlights the power of determination and devotion to one's craft.

- The consequences of envy and favouritism – Duryodhana's jealousy and his intervention to make Karṇa a prince to spite Arjuna demonstrates how envy can lead to manipulation and decisions that have long-lasting consequences. It also emphasizes the importance of fairness and integrity in leadership.

- The importance of keeping one's promise – Ekalavya's willingness to sacrifice his thumb, which was integral to his skill, just to keep his word of offering whatever guru-dakṣiṇā Droṇācārya desired, is a profound example.

- The need for patience – The postponement of the duel between Karṇa and Arjuna illustrates the value of patience. The situation was resolved with a delay, teaching that sometimes things must unfold in their own time, even when emotions and passions run high.

Values reflected

- Self-discipline (tapas) – Ekalavya's and Arjuna's relentless practice and the efforts of the Kuru princes in their training under Droṇācārya demonstrate the importance of focus and commitment.

- Humility (vinaya) – Ekalavya's sacrifice of his thumb is a lesson in humility and respect for one's teachers and the path of learning.

- Courage (dhairya) – Karṇa's boldness to challenge Arjuna despite being an outsider, and Arjuna's own calm composure in his skills, show courage and confidence in one's abilities.

- Wisdom (viveka) – The thoughtful response of Kṛpācārya in trying to maintain order and discipline in the competition highlights wisdom and discretion in leadership.

7. Duryodhana's jealousy and the murderous conspiracy

The Pāṇḍavas were growing stronger, and their virtues were becoming well-known. Bhīṣma advised Dhṛtarāṣṭra, "Yudhiṣṭhira should be the next king of Hastināpura. He is wise, noble, and just."

But Duryodhana was filled with jealousy. He could not bear the thought of the Pāṇḍavas gaining power. One day, he went to his father with a plan. "Father, let us send the Pāṇḍavas to the Paśupati fair at Vāraṇāvata. It will keep them away from the kingdom for a while."

Then Duryodhana, his brother Duhśāsana, Karṇa, and Śakuni who was Gāndhārī's brother, formed an evil conspiracy. With the sanction of Dhṛtarāṣṭra, Duryodhana ordered his ally, Purocana, to build a palace at Vāraṇāvata made of highly flammable materials. The plan was to burn Kuntī and the Pāṇḍavas alive while they slept.

The wise Vidura, the Pāṇḍavas' well-wisher, learned of Duryodhana's plot. He rushed to Yudhiṣṭhira. "There is danger at Vāraṇāvata. Duryodhana intends to kill you."

Yudhiṣṭhira did not want to alarm anyone, so he kept calm. "We do have the power to go against Duryodhana who has the support of the king, his father. We will handle this quietly."

Vidura sent a miner to dig a secret tunnel beneath the palace. The tunnel would allow the Pāṇḍavas to escape into the forest if the palace caught fire.

That night, when the fire was set, Bhīma quickly bolted Purocana's room from the outside, trapping him inside. As the palace caught fire, the Pāṇḍavas escaped through the tunnel into the forest.

The people of Vāraṇāvata tried to put out the flames, but the fire was too intense. By the time they arrived, the palace had burned to the ground, and everyone believed the Pāṇḍavas had perished in the flames.

Lessons to be learned

- Wisdom and courage in the face of adversity – The Pāṇḍavas handled the situation with calm wisdom. Despite the grave threat to their lives, they did not panic and acted strategically to escape. This highlights the value of wisdom (viveka) in difficult situations, as well as the importance of courage (dhairya) to face threats.

- Gratitude and loyalty – Vidura's quick action in helping the Pāṇḍavas demonstrates a deep sense of loyalty and gratitude. His dedication to their safety, despite the danger, shows gratitude (kṛtajñatā) and compassion (dayā) for the Pāṇḍavas' well-being.

Values reflected

- Wisdom (viveka): Yudhiṣṭhira's calm and thoughtful approach to danger shows wisdom.

- Courage (dhairya): The Pāṇḍavas' bravery in facing the life-threatening situation and managing their escape demonstrates courage.

- Gratitude (kṛtajñatā): Vidura's loyalty to the Pāṇḍavas and his prompt action reflect a deep sense of gratitude and responsibility.

- Compassion (dayā): Vidura's compassion is evident in his desire to save the Pāṇḍavas from harm.

8. Escape into the forest

Bhīma, the possessor of supreme strength, carried his mother and brothers and ran swiftly in the forest. After going for miles through the forest, the Pāṇḍavas, weary and hungry, rested under a banyan tree. Bhīma went to fetch water, and when he returned, he found his brothers and mother fast asleep.

Nearby, a rākṣasa5 named Hiḍimba, who lived in the forest with his sister Hiḍimbā, smelled the presence of humans. "Sister," he said, "Go and bring us some fresh prey."

Hiḍimbā went to find the intruders. Upon seeing Bhīma, her heart changed. She fell in love with his mighty form and transforming herself into a beautiful maiden, she approached Bhīma. "Who are you? What brings you to these dangerous woods?" she said.

Bhīma explained their situation, and Hiḍimbā, moved by their plight, promised to help them.

However, her brother Hiḍimba soon appeared, furious. "What is this? You've fallen in love with your prey?" he roared.

Hiḍimba, uprooting a mighty tree, challenged Bhīma to a fight. But Bhīma was more than a match for him. Using his immense strength, Bhīma soon defeated Hiḍimba and killed him.

Hiḍimbā then said, "I now have no one left in this world. O noble Bhīma, please marry me and give me your protection." Bhīma replied, "I will marry you on two conditions. First, my

---

5 *Belonging to or like an evil spirit, demoniacal, possessing a demon's nature (Apte: The Practical Sanskrit-English Dictionary)*

mother needs to approve of this marriage. Second, I can only stay with you till our son is born. As soon as he is born, I shall move on. We still have to find a way to get our rightful kingdom back." Hiḍimbā agreed.

Kuntī, impressed by Hiḍimbā's character, agreed to the match. Bhīma and Hiḍimbā were married, and soon they had a son named Ghaṭotkaca, a mighty warrior like his father. Once Ghaṭotkaca was born, Bhīma moved on with the Pāṇḍavas

9. Life in Ekacakra

The Pāṇḍavas continued to hide in the forest. After some time, they decided to leave their hiding place and move to a nearby village called Ekacakra. Disguised as Brāhmaṇas, they stayed with a kind brāhmaṇa family, living by begging alms and chanting prayers.

One day, Kuntī overheard the brāhmaṇa family in distress. "What is troubling you?" she asked.

The brāhmaṇa explained, "This village is under the curse of a demon named Bakāsura. Every day, a cartload of food is sent to him, but the demon demands a life in return. We've lost many lives this way. Tomorrow it's the turn of our family to sacrifice a member."

Kuntī immediately understood the family's predicament. "I will send my son Bhīma to defeat the demon. He is strong enough to destroy him."

Bhīma agreed without hesitation. He drove the cart with all the food to the cave of the demon and then proceeded to eat all the food. Seeing this Bakāsura was incensed and challenged him to a fight. After a mighty battle, Bhīma killed the demon. He dragged the demon's body back to the village for all to see.

The villagers rejoiced, and the brāhmaṇa family was immensely grateful.

Lessons to be learned

- Courage and action – Bhīma's immediate decision to confront the demon Bakāsura demonstrates courage (dhairya) and the willingness to act in the face of danger to protect others. This teaches us that true courage is not just about physical strength but also about acting decisively when others are in need.

- Compassion and helpfulness – Kuntī's quick understanding of the situation and her decision to send Bhīma to help the brāhmaṇa family showcases compassion (dayā) and a deep sense of responsibility for the welfare of others. She shows that helping those in need is essential, especially when one has the means to help.

Values reflected

- Courage (dhairya) – Bhīma's bravery in facing the demon without hesitation.

- Compassion (dayā) – Kuntī's empathetic response to the brāhmaṇa family's plight.

10. The Svayaṁvara of Draupadī

After his defeat at the Pāṇḍavas' hands at the behest of Droṇa, King Drupada was so impressed with Arjuna's skill and valour that he decided to get his daughter, Draupadī who was extremely renowned for her beauty and grace, married to Arjuna. When he heard that the Pāṇḍavas had perished in the fire, he was heart-broken. However, soon he began to heard rumours that the Pāṇḍavas were actually alive and in hiding. Hoping to draw them out, Drupada decided to host a svayaṁvara for Draupadī. A svayaṁvara (meaning, self-choice) is a practice allowed to kṣatrīya girls where the girl, as a bride, chooses her husband from a group of suitors.

The story of Draupadī and her twin brother, Dhṛṣṭadyumna's birth is very interesting. After Drupada was defeated by the Pāṇḍavas as guru-dakṣiṇā for Droṇa, Drupada was seething with anger and shame. He decided to perform a sacrifice for a son who could kill Droṇa. From the sacrificial fire appeared Dhṛṣṭadyumna, who possessed the splendour of Agni himself. The mighty hero was born with bow in hand for the destruction of Droṇa. Immediately after him came Kṛṣṇā or Draupadī, resplendent like the fire, possessing bright features and magnificent beauty.

Upon hearing about the svayaṁvara, the Pāṇḍavas decided that an alliance with Drupada would help their cause in getting Hastinapura back. Therefore, disguised as brāhmaṇas, the Pāṇḍavas attended the ceremony to try and win the beautiful

Draupadī. There were many kings and princes present who had come to win the hand of Draupadī including, Duryodhana and his brothers, Karṇa, Śakuni, Śiśupāla, Jarāsandha and others. Lord Kṛṣṇa with his sons, Lord Balarāma and other Yādavas were also present. Everyone present was stunned by Draupadī's beauty and wanted her as his wife.

At the svayaṁvara, Draupadī's brother, Dhṛṣṭadyumna, explained the challenge. "Here is a mighty bow that you must string. Then you must shoot five arrows through that tiny hole high up above to hit the target beyond it," he said.

Many princes tried but were tossed and flung about just trying to string the bow. Karṇa successfully strung the bow but Draupadī, exercising her right to choose, said that she would not marry the son of a sūta.

Kṛṣṇa had seen and recognised the Pāṇḍavas. He therefore silently bid his sons and other Yādavas to remain seated as spectators.

When all the kings had finished trying, Arjuna, still in his brāhmaṇa disguise, stood up. The crowd gasped to see such a handsome and powerful bodied brāhmaṇa. Arjuna picked up the bow, easily strung it, aimed, and shot the arrows at the target bringing it down. The other brāhmaṇas erupted in joy waving their upper cloths above their heads. Draupadī, filled with joy, walked over and garlanded Arjuna, accepting him as her husband.

The kings were stunned. "Who is this brāhmaṇa?" they said. "How can a brāhmaṇa be a better archer than any of us?"

All the defeated monarchs took up their arms and rushed to
kill the Pāṇḍavas. But Bhīma tore up a massive tree and
protected his brothers and Draupadī. This was watched by Lord
Kṛṣṇa and the Yadus with great satisfaction.

When the Pāṇḍavas returned to the hut they shared, mother
Kuntī thinking they had brought back alms, told them to "share"
whatever they had brought. The brothers, in order to respect their
mother's words, each decided to marry Draupadī. Kṛṣṇa and
Vyāsadeva who came there at that time, supported this, saying it
was part of their unique destiny. So, all five Pāṇḍavas married
Draupadī.

11. The Pāṇḍavas return to Hastināpura

The Pāṇḍavas were now famous. Realising that they were still alive, Dhṛtarāṣṭra invited them back to Hastināpura. They returned, much to the joy of the people who believed them dead. Duryodhana, frustrated, knew the Pāṇḍavas had survived but waited for the right moment to strike.

To satisfy Duryodhana, Dhṛtarāṣṭra divided the kingdom into two parts. All the barren land of Khāṇḍavaprastha along with the Khāṇḍava forest was given to the Pāṇḍavas while the Kauravas held on to the cities and palaces. On this arid land, the Pāṇḍavas worked hard to build a stunning city and named it Indraprastha after Indra who was the protecting deity of the land.

It was a well-planned city. For protection it was surrounded by a huge moat and a high wall was erected. There were double gates at the entrance. The turrets were stocked full of varied weapons that could kill hundreds of enemies in one shot. It had huge mansions adorning it. Indraprastha was now the official residence and kingdom of the Pāṇḍavas.

The people loved their new king, and peace seemed to reign.

Lessons to be learned

- Courage in adversity, adaptability and hard work – Despite being given barren land, the Pāṇḍavas transformed it into the magnificent city of Indraprastha, teaching us to face challenges with determination and creativity.

- Forgiveness and diplomacy – By accepting Dhṛtarāṣṭra's offer despite past wrongs, the Pāṇḍavas show the value of forgiveness and the ability to work toward peace.

Values reflected

- Respect (ādara): Shown in the Pāṇḍavas' adherence to their elder, Dhṛtarāṣṭra's instructions even when the instructions were not favourable to them.

- Wisdom (viveka): Seen in their acceptance of Khāṇḍavaprastha and their efforts to develop it into Indraprastha.

- Patience (titikṣā) and courage (dhairya): Demonstrated in their perseverance in transforming barren land into a prosperous city.

- Self-discipline (tapas): Displayed in their restraint and strategic approach toward building their kingdom and maintaining peace.

12. The Code of Conduct and Arjuna's exile

To maintain marital harmony, the sage Nārada advised the Pāṇḍavas to draw up a code of conduct. Each brother would have exclusive time with Draupadī, and anyone who broke the rule would go on a pilgrimage for twelve years.

One day, a brāhmaṇa came to Arjuna, claiming that thieves had stolen his cows. Arjuna, eager to help, realized his weapons were locked in Draupadī's chamber, where Yudhiṣṭhira was spending his time with her.

In a moment of conflict, Arjuna decided to violate the code. He entered Draupadī's chamber, retrieved his weapons, and set out to rescue the cows.

When Arjuna returned, he immediately went to Yudhiṣṭhira and confessed his mistake. "I broke our agreement. Please allow me to go on my pilgrimage for twelve years," he said.

Yudhiṣṭhira, though reluctant, understood. "You did it for the good of the people," he said, but Arjuna insisted on upholding the code. Thus, he left for the forest to fulfil his vow.

Arjuna's first stop was the Himālayas, where he spent time with sages, learned from them, and performed religious rituals to strengthen his spiritual resolve.

One day, while Arjuna was by the river, a beautiful woman appeared before him. She was Ulūpī, the daughter of the Nāga king who ruled over the serpent kingdom under the waters. She had heard of Arjuna's great qualities, and when she saw him, she immediately fell in love with him.

Without hesitation, she decided to abduct him.

As Arjuna prepared for a bath in the river, Ulūpī emerged from the water, grabbed him, and pulled him under the surface. Arjuna, startled, demanded, "What is this? Where are you taking me?"

Ulūpī, with a calm smile, responded, "I am Ulūpī, the daughter of Kauravya, born in the line of Airāvata of the Nāga kingdom. I am filled with desire for you and have brought you here to marry me."

Arjuna was taken aback but seeing no way to resist, he agreed. He stayed with Ulūpī in her underwater palace for that night. The next day she took him back to the land and left him there. She also granted him a boon. "You shall be able to vanquish any water creature," she said.

The king welcomed him warmly, and Arjuna decided to stay for a while. While there, he saw Citravāhana's daughter, Citraṅgadā, and was immediately struck by her beauty.

He went to Citravāhana and asked, "Will you give me your daughter, Citraṅgadā's hand in marriage?"

Citravāhana was pleased but replied, "Citraṅgadā is my only child, and I have no other heirs. If you wish to marry her, you must agree that her son will be the crown prince of my kingdom."

Arjuna, though surprised, agreed to the condition. He married Citraṅgadā, and soon a son, Babhruvāhana, was born. Citravāhana, as promised, adopted the child as his heir. After that, Arjuna bid farewell and continued his journey.

Arjuna travelled southward, eventually reaching the coast near Purī. Here, he spent time with sages, and they complained about the ferocious crocodiles infesting the nearby waters, making it hard for them to bathe. Arjuna promised to help and leaped into the water, determined to remove the threat.

But as he entered the water, a massive crocodile caught his leg. Arjuna, with great strength, pulled the creature from the water. To his astonishment, the crocodile transformed into a beautiful apsarā.

"Who are you?" Arjuna asked, bewildered.

The apsarā, bowing, explained, "Long ago, my friends and I offended a sage. As punishment, we were cursed to live as crocodiles. The sage, however, said that we would be freed only when a virtuous warrior, like you, would pull us from the water. Thank you for saving us."

Arjuna, moved by her story, helped her release the other crocodiles. Each transformed back into a heavenly maiden, and they thanked him before disappearing to their celestial home.

After this, Arjuna made his way to Dvārakā, where he was warmly received by Kṛṣṇa and his brother Balarāma. During his stay, Arjuna saw Kṛṣṇa's sister Subhadrā, and he fell in love with her. She too reciprocated his feelings.

When Arjuna confided in Kṛṣṇa about his feelings for Subhadrā, Kṛṣṇa thoughtfully replied, "Balarāma has already decided that Subhadrā should marry Duryodhana, and he will not consent to your union with her. The best course of action is for you to elope with Subhadrā."

Arjuna obtained Yudhiṣṭhira's permission for this course of action. He then borrowed Kṛṣṇa's chariot and, when Subhadrā was returning from the temple, he abducted her. Subhadrā, who had also fallen in love with Arjuna, smilingly went with him.

Balarāma, furious at the abduction, rushed to Kṛṣṇa, demanding an explanation. "This is disgraceful! How could you, my own brother, allow Arjuna to dishonour us like this?"

Kṛṣṇa, calm as always, responded, "Balarāma, do not be angry. The Pāṇḍavas are strong allies, and Arjuna is invincible. If we fight him, we risk defeat. Instead, let us honourably invite Arjuna back and arrange for his marriage to Subhadrā."

Realizing the wisdom of Kṛṣṇa's words, Balarāma agreed, and the royal wedding between Arjuna and Subhadrā was arranged.

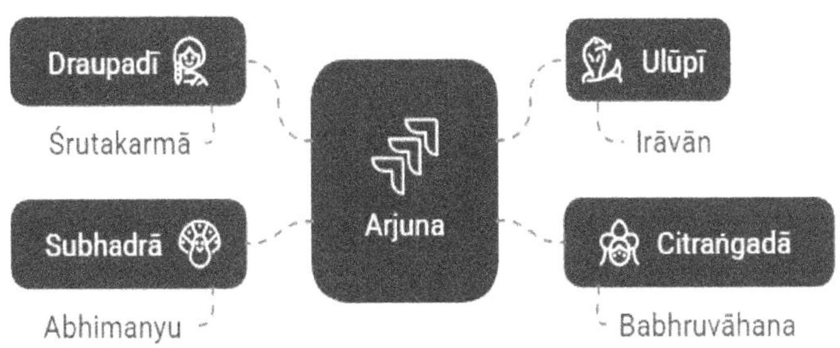

After the wedding, Arjuna returned to Indraprastha with Subhadrā, where he was joyfully reunited with his brothers. Subhadrā humbly approached Draupadī and, touching her feet, said, "Sister, please accept me as your maid."

Draupadī, initially upset by the situation, was won over by Subhadrā's humility and accepted her with open arms.

From his four wives, Arjuna had four sons. Śrutakarmā from Draupadī, Irāvān from Ulūpī, Babhruvāhana from Citrangadā and Abhimanyu from Subhadrā. All his sons were fierce and renowned warriors.

Lessons to be learned

- Upholding integrity and taking responsibility – Arjuna's adherence to the code of conduct, even after breaking it for a noble cause, demonstrates the importance of accepting responsibility for one's actions.

- Compassion and problem-solving – Arjuna's encounter with the sages and the cursed apsarās teaches us to use our strength and abilities for the benefit of others.

- Humility and forgiveness in relationships – Subhadrā's humility in approaching Draupadī and Draupadī's eventual acceptance of her show the importance of humility (vinaya) and forgiveness (kṣamā) in maintaining harmony in relationships.

- Strategic wisdom and diplomacy – Kṛṣṇa's advice to Arjuna about eloping with Subhadrā demonstrates the importance of wisdom (viveka) and strategic thinking in resolving conflicts without unnecessary harm.

Values reflected

- Respect (ādara): Shown by Subhadrā's respectful approach to Draupadī.

- Truthfulness (satya): Arjuna's honest confession about breaking the code.

- Compassion (dayā/karuṇā): Helping the nymphs and sages.

- Self-discipline (tapas): Arjuna's insistence on completing his exile.

- Humility (vinaya): Subhadrā's attitude toward Draupadī.

- Forgiveness (kṣamā): Draupadī's acceptance of Subhadrā.

- Courage (dhairya): Arjuna's readiness to face

challenges, such as rescuing cows and confronting crocodiles.

- Wisdom (viveka): Kṛṣṇa's diplomatic handling of Subhadrā's marriage. 55

13. The Rājasūya yajña of Yudhiṣṭhira

One day, Kṛṣṇa and Arjuna were talking when a brāhmaṇa approached them. He introduced himself as Agni, the fire-god, and explained his hunger for meat. "I've tried to burn the Khāṇḍava forest many times, but Indra, the god of rain, always extinguishes the fire," Agni said. "I need your help to stall Indra and allow me to consume the forest."

Kṛṣṇa and Arjuna agreed to assist. Agni, with his divine power, provided them with celestial weapons. Together, they set the forest ablaze, and as expected, Indra rushed to stop them. But Kṛṣṇa and Arjuna successfully held Indra at bay.

During the fire, an asura, fleeing the flames, sought refuge with Arjuna. "Please protect me," the asura pleaded.

At Arjuna's request, Agni let the asura go. The asura, who revealed himself to be Maya, the architect of the asuras, offered to build something for Arjuna and Kṛṣṇa in return for his life. "I can create the most beautiful palace hall for you," Maya promised.

Kṛṣṇa accepted, and soon, the Pāṇḍavas' palace hall in Indraprastha was complete in fourteen months. It was a marvel of beauty, shining so brilliantly that it seemed to outshine even the sun. It was constructed with the finest materials, and had golden walls, archways, and exquisite paintings. Guarded by eight thousand fierce Rākṣasas, it featured a unique tank filled with jewelled lotuses, golden fish, crystal-clear water and adorned all around with jewels and precious stones; many people mistook it for land and fell into it with eyes open. Pearl-studded marble banks and crystal stairs led to its edge, where fragrant breezes gently stirred the blossoms. Surrounded by lush trees, artificial woods, and tanks with waterfowl, the palace provided a haven of beauty and tranquillity for the Pāṇḍavas.

To establish dharma and protect all people, Yudhiṣṭhira, at the bidding of the sage Nārada, decided to perform the Rājasūya yajña. This yajña is a great sacrifice performed by a supreme sovereign at the time of his coronation to confirm his sovereignty.

The only king who refused to acknowledge Yudhiṣṭhira's supremacy was Jarāsandha, the powerful ruler of Magadha. Ambitious and wicked, Jarāsandha aspired to perform the Rājasūya yajña himself. As part of his dark plan, he had abducted eighty six kings with an intention to sacrifice hundred kings in total, to complete his ritual. His defiance and malevolence posed a great obstacle to Yudhiṣṭhira's path to establishing his supremacy. To fulfil his righteous goal, it became imperative for Yudhiṣṭhira to confront and defeat Jarāsandha.

At Kṛṣṇa's advice, Yudhiṣṭhira sent Bhīma, Arjuna, and Kṛṣṇa to Magadha to persuade Jarāsandha to submit to his sovereignty.

Jarāsandha however refused to submit. "I will fight one of you in a duel," Jarāsandha declared.

Bhīma stepped forward to face him, and after a long and brutal battle, Bhīma defeated Jarāsandha, tearing his body in half, using the secret Kṛṣṇa had shared with him.

With Jarāsandha's death, the kings he had imprisoned were freed, and they swore allegiance to the Pāṇḍavas. Then, Yudhiṣṭhira sent his brothers in all four directions to conquer the kingdoms there. Almost all the kings accepted the supremacy of Yudhiṣṭhira. Those kings who opposed them were defeated.

The Rājasūya yajña was completed with great fanfare, and Kṛṣṇa was venerated as the first guest of honour by all. However, Śiśupāla, Kṛṣṇa's cousin, was filled with jealousy and insulted Kṛṣṇa publicly. Kṛṣṇa, having endured over a hundred insults, finally ended Śiśupāla's life with his disc, the Sudarśana cakra.

Lessons to be learned

- Righteous leadership and duty – Yudhiṣṭhira's decision to perform the Rājasūya yajña highlights the importance of establishing dharma through righteous leadership. A just ruler serves as a protector of the people and upholds moral values.

- Wisdom in decision-making – Kṛṣṇa's guidance throughout – whether in managing Jarāsandha or navigating Śiśupāla's insults – demonstrates the importance of wisdom and strategic thinking in achieving goals without compromising ethics.

- Courage and determination – Bhīma's duel with Jarāsandha exemplifies bravery and the resolve to overcome formidable challenges for a righteous cause.

- Self-restraint and forgiveness – Kṛṣṇa's patience with Śiśupāla's insults teaches the value of tolerance and forgiveness, enduring provocations until a line of righteousness is crossed.

- Gratitude and loyalty – The loyalty of the freed kings and their allegiance to Yudhiṣṭhira reflect the importance of gratitude and mutual respect in leadership.

Values reflected

- Courage (dhairya): Bhīma's fierce battle with Jarāsandha.

- Wisdom (viveka): Kṛṣṇa's strategic counsel to Yudhiṣṭhira and Bhīma.

- Patience (titikṣā): Kṛṣṇa's endurance of Śiśupāla's insults.

- Respect (ādara): Honouring Śrī Kṛṣṇa as the first guest of the yajña.

- Gratitude (kṛtajñatā): The freed kings' allegiance to Yudhiṣṭhira.

- Self-discipline (tapas): The Pāṇḍavas' restraint and commitment during their conquests.

- Truthfulness (satya): Upholding dharma through honest and just actions.

14. Duryodhana's anger

Duryodhana, still envious of the Pāṇḍavas' prosperity, stayed on after the Rājasūya yajña at the newly built palace in Indraprastha. He saw many celestial designs that were not available in Hastināpura. He was also mesmerised by its illusions.

One day, while King Duryodhana was exploring the marvellous hall built by Maya, the Mayasabhā, he came upon a crystal surface. Mistaking it for water, he lifted his garments to avoid getting them wet. Realizing his mistake, he continued wandering through the grand halls, visibly perplexed. Later, upon encountering a clear lake adorned with crystal lotuses, he assumed it was solid ground and fell in, fully clothed.

Witnessing Duryodhana's mishap, Bhīma and others present could not help but laugh at the unintended humour of the situation. The palace servants promptly brought dry and elegant clothing for the king. As Duryodhana moved through the intricate palace, he mistook an open crystal door for a closed one and struck his head, becoming momentarily disoriented. Similarly, he mistook a closed door for an open one and reached out, only to stumble. These repeated confusions, caused by the extraordinary craftsmanship of the palace, left Duryodhana flustered.

Eventually, after taking leave of the Pāṇḍavas and marvelling at the splendour of the Rājasūya sacrifice, Duryodhana returned to Hastināpura, his mind weighed down by the grandeur he had witnessed and angered by his many embarrassments within the palace.

15. All is lost

Now that Duryodhana had seen that the Pāṇḍavas had worked hard to transform their arid lands into palaces that were more beautiful than his own, he wanted the entire kingdom for himself. His jealousy and covetousness festered, and he plotted with his maternal uncle, Śakuni to ruin the Pāṇḍavas.

Śakuni, with his cunning mind, devised a plan to invite Yudhiṣṭhira to a game of dice. "Yudhiṣṭhira loves the game," Śakuni said. "None can beat me because I use charmed dice. Let us use the game to take everything from him."

Duryodhana carried out the plan, persuading his father, Dhṛtarāṣṭra, to invite Yudhiṣṭhira to a game of dice. At first Yudhiṣṭhira refused saying that gambling was against the principles of dharma. However, Śakuni began taunting him saying, "Gambling is just another form of contest like a sparring competition. You appear to be afraid of losing and so you are refusing to face me."

At being challenged thus, Yudhiṣṭhira, proud and unable to back down6, accepted. He soon lost everything – his kingdom,

---

[6]Yudhiṣṭhira, being dharma-rājā, knew the consequences of playing dice. He knew that such games bring downfall. But he trusted that since Dhṛtarāṣṭra was there, nothing bad could happen. He also did not want to disrespect his elders by refusing their request. Moreover, being a kṣatrīya, he couldn't decline the offer since a game of dice was considered equal to a challenge to war, and it would have been considered a regression of his dharma. He knew that Śakuni was cheating, but the more he lost, the more he lost his mental stability and sanity. He was desperate to win back all he had lost and, in the process, lost his

his brothers, and even himself. Finally, goaded by Śakuni, Yudhiṣṭhira staked Queen Draupadī – and lost her too!

At this, the Kauravas and Karṇa laughed loudly while everyone else in the court sat aghast. Duryodhana ordered that Draupadī should now live as a maid amongst the other maids of the Palace. He ordered a messenger to bring her to the court so that she could be given her instructions.

When Draupadī refused to come with the messenger, Duhśāsana went into her chambers and dragged a bent Draupadī into the court by her hair, shouting "Slave! Slave! Come along!"

---

wisdom and his sense of discernment between right and wrong, and forgot Lord Kṛṣṇa.
This is why Śrī Kṛṣṇa says in Bhagavad Gītā 10.36: dyūtaṁ chalayatāmasmi – I am the gambling of the cheats and the splendor of the splendid. Gambling is a dangerous vice that ruins families, businesses, and lives. It may be argued that it was Yudhiṣṭhira's weakness for gambling that led to the Mahābhārata war.

The piece of cloth she was dressed in was half loosened by her being dragged in. Draupadī was praying piteously to Kṛṣṇa.

The Kuru elders did not help her, and she was humiliated. Karṇa taunted the Pāṇḍavas, and Duryodhana ordered Draupadī to sit on his lap, a final insult.

Bhīma, unable to bear it, vowed, "I will break Duryodhana's thigh for this insult." Draupadī, in her humiliation, condemned the elders for their inaction, and Dhṛtarāṣṭra, realizing the consequences, sought to offer a way out.

"Duryodhana, you must release the Pāṇḍavas after thirteen years of exile," Dhṛtarāṣṭra declared, "and they must remain incognito during the final year. If their identity is discovered, they will have to go into exile again."

Taking Kuntī's blessing, the Pāṇḍavas prepared for their exile. Yudhiṣṭhira prayed to the Sun god, who gave Draupadī a miraculous copper plate that would provide endless food till Draupadī ate her meal. This helped the Pāṇḍavas through their hard times in the forest, and soon the Pāṇḍavas began inviting all sages and saints to share food with them.

Lessons from the Bhagavad Gītā 2.62-63

The verses from Bhagavad Gītā 2.62-63 state:

dhyāyato viṣayān puṁsaḥ saṅgas teṣūpajāyate
saṅgāt sañjāyate kāmaḥ kāmāt krodho 'bhijāyate

While contemplating the objects of the senses, a person develops attachment for them, and from such attachment lust develops, and from lust anger arises.

krodhād bhavati sammohaḥ sammohāt smṛti-vibhramaḥ

smṛti-bhraṁśād buddhi-nāśo buddhi-nāśāt praṇaśyati

From anger, complete delusion arises, and from delusion bewilderment of memory. When memory is bewildered, intelligence is lost, and when intelligence is lost one is ruined.

The verses 2.62 and 2.63 provide a sequential analysis of how uncontrolled attachment (dhyāna) to sense objects leads to a chain reaction culminating in self-destruction:

1. Contemplation (dhyāna) on sense objects leads to attachment (saṅga).

2. Attachment develops into desire (kāma).

3. Desire, when unfulfilled, gives rise to anger (krodha).

4. Anger causes delusion (sammoha).

5. Delusion disrupts memory (smṛti-vibhramaḥ).

6. Loss of memory leads to loss of discernment (buddhi-nāśa).

7. The loss of discernment results in ruin (praṇaśyati).

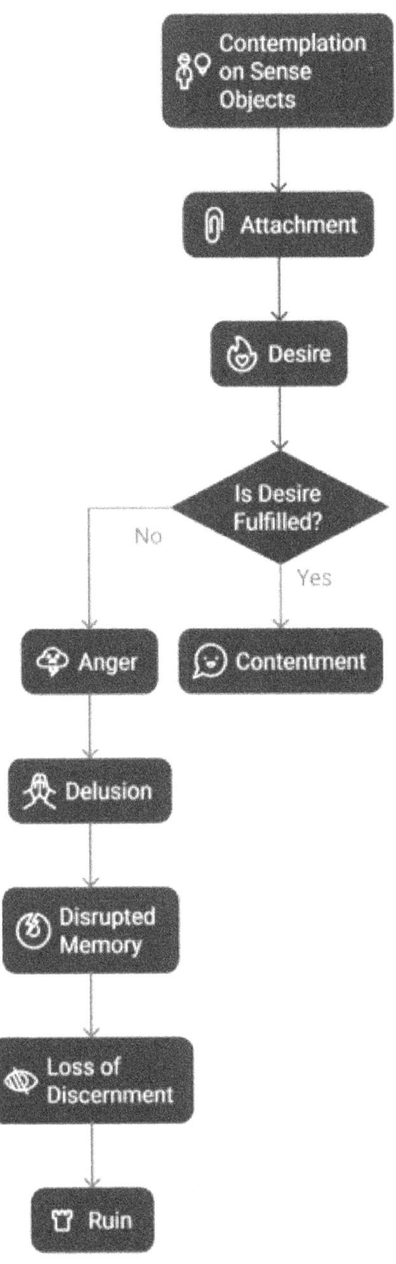

Contemplation on Sense Objects
Attachment
Desire
Is Desire Fulfilled?
No
Yes
Anger
Contentment
Delusion
Disrupted Memory
Loss of Discernment
Ruin

Application to Duryodhana

The sequence described in BG 2.62–2.63 is exemplified in Duryodhana's reaction to his humiliation at the Mayasabhā, where he fell into an illusionary pool of water created by Maya Dānava. Here is how Duryodhana's response follows this destructive progression:

1. Contemplation (dhyāna) on sense objects:

Duryodhana had been obsessively contemplating the grandeur of the Pāṇḍavas' newfound wealth and power, symbolized by the grand Mayasabhā and the palace. His envy and fixation on their prosperity began to consume his thoughts, leading to attachment.

2. Attachment (saṅga):

This attachment to his sense of superiority and entitlement to the throne created a deep-seated jealousy toward the Pāṇḍavas. His inability to accept their success further entrenched his emotions.

3. Desire (kāma):

Duryodhana's attachment gave rise to an intense desire to outshine and defeat the Pāṇḍavas. He longed to humiliate them and reclaim his perceived superiority.

4. Anger (krodha):

When Duryodhana fell into the illusionary pool, his desire for dominance was thwarted, triggering a surge of anger. His perceived humiliation in front of the assembled guests became unbearable.

5. Delusion (sammoha):

Overwhelmed by anger, Duryodhana's thinking became clouded. Instead of reflecting on his actions or seeking reconciliation, he was consumed by delusions of enmity. He began to see the Pāṇḍavas as his mortal enemies, blaming them for his humiliation.

6. Memory disruption (smṛti-vibhramaḥ):

Delusion disrupted Duryodhana's memory of dharma, the ethical and moral principles he was expected to uphold as a prince. He forgot the values of kinship, righteousness, and fairness.

7. Loss of discernment (buddhi-nāśa):

With his sense of judgment impaired, Duryodhana resorted to underhanded schemes like the dice game to undermine the Pāṇḍavas. His inability to discern the consequences of his actions led him further away from righteousness.

8. Ruin (praṇaśyati):

Ultimately, this chain of events culminated in Duryodhana's downfall. His relentless anger and jealousy not only destroyed his spiritual potential but also led to the catastrophic Kurukṣetra war, resulting in his death and the decimation of his lineage.

Application to Yudhiṣṭhira's behaviour in the dice game

The Bhagavad Gītā verses 2.62–2.63 outline how attachment to sense objects leads to a destructive sequence:

1. Contemplation (dhyāna) leads to attachment (saṅga):

Yudhiṣṭhira, though a dharmic king, was fascinated by the idea of honour and proving his superiority through gambling. His attachment to upholding his pride as a Kṣatriya and his belief in playing fairly under challenge made him susceptible to entering the game of dice, even though he was aware of its dangers.

2. Attachment develops into desire (kāma):

Once in the game, Yudhiṣṭhira's attachment to the idea of winning and reclaiming his honor transformed into a strong desire to prove himself. This desire made him gamble increasingly large stakes, including his kingdom, his brothers, and eventually Draupadī. His inability to detach from the allure of victory fuelled his recklessness.

3. Desire, when unfulfilled, gives rise to anger (krodha):

As he repeatedly lost, frustration began to cloud Yudhiṣṭhira's judgment. While he did not openly express anger, his inner turmoil led him to make desperate wagers, which showed an increasing lack of self-control.

4. Anger causes delusion (sammoha):

Yudhiṣṭhira's anger – at his losses, the deceitful tactics of Śakuni, and his inability to stop himself – gave way to delusion. He became blind to the ethical boundaries of the game, staking his family and Draupadī without considering the moral implications or consequences of his actions.

5. Delusion disrupts memory (smṛti-vibhramaḥ):

In his delusion, Yudhiṣṭhira forgot his responsibilities as a husband, brother, and king. His memory of dharma – especially the principle of protecting those dependent on him – was obscured by his obsession with the game.

6. Loss of discernment (buddhi-nāśa):

With his judgment impaired, Yudhiṣṭhira continued gambling recklessly, disregarding the warnings of his brothers and the inevitable downfall he was orchestrating. His inability to discern right from wrong in the heat of the moment led to catastrophic consequences.

7. Ruin (praṇaśyati):

While Yudhiṣṭhira did not face complete spiritual ruin due to his repentance and eventual redemption, his actions during the dice game caused immense suffering to his family, dishonour to Draupadī, and the loss of their kingdom. The humiliation and turmoil sowed the seeds for the Kurukṣetra war.

Reflection

Yudhiṣṭhira's descent during the dice game serves as a powerful example of how even a righteous person can be ensnared by the cycle described in BG 2.62–2.63. It underscores the importance of vigilance in managing the mind and desires. Bhakti teaches that surrender to Kṛṣṇa and cultivating attachment to His service can help transcend such weaknesses and safeguard against the destructive progression outlined in these verses.

Message in the context of Kṛṣṇa-bhakti

Bhakti teaches the importance of engaging the mind and senses to cultivate spiritual progress and devotion to Kṛṣṇa:

1. Avoiding material attachment:

The philosophy emphasizes renunciation of material desires, as attachment to sense objects detracts from devotion. This is aligned with BG 2.62–63, which warn of the consequences of unchecked desires.

2. Embracing humility and patience:

Unlike Duryodhana, devotees are encouraged to cultivate humility (vinaya) and patience (titikṣā). Bhakti advocates introspection and remembrance of Kṛṣṇa (smaraṇa) to avoid the pitfalls of anger and delusion.

3. Staying centered on Kṛṣṇa:

The philosophy teaches that attachment to Kṛṣṇa's lotus feet transforms one's desires into spiritual aspirations. By engaging in devotional practices, one replaces harmful emotions like anger with joy (ānanda) and compassion (dayā).

Conclusion

BG 2.62–63 exemplifies how unchecked desires and anger lead to one's downfall, both, material and spiritual, as vividly illustrated by Duryodhana's life. Bhakti offers a solution by guiding individuals to shift their focus from material attachments to spiritual devotion, ensuring they avoid the destructive cycle described in the Gītā and exemplified in the Mahābhārata.

Lessons to be learned

- The dangers of envy – Duryodhana's jealousy of the Pāṇḍavas' success led to devastating consequences.

- The power of forgiveness and patience – Despite her humiliation, Draupadī displayed remarkable restraint. The Pāṇḍavas, too, accepted exile with patience and focused on preparing for the future rather than succumbing to despair.

- Righteousness always prevails – Dhṛtarāṣtra's decision to grant the Pāṇḍavas exile with conditions, though flawed, reaffirmed the idea that even in adversity, dharma can guide towards a better outcome – freedom in exile as against a life in slavery to the evil Kauravas.

Values reflected

- Respect (ādara): Draupadī's expectation of protection from the elders reflects respect for dharma and societal roles.

- Patience (titikṣā): The Pāṇḍavas endured exile with steadfastness, maintaining their resolve.

- Self-discipline (tapas): Yudhiṣṭhira's devotion to dharma and the Pāṇḍavas' restraint during their hardships display self-discipline.

- Courage (dhairya): Bhīma's vow and the Pāṇḍavas' determination to face the challenges of exile highlight bravery.

- Gratitude (kṛtajñatā): Yudhiṣṭhira's prayer to the Sun god and the reverence for the miraculous copper plate underscore gratitude for divine assistance.

16. Kṛṣṇa's anger

When Kṛṣṇa heard about what had transpired from Sātyakī, he quickly came to visit the Pāṇḍavas in the forest.

The plight of his noble cousins shook him to the core. "Duryodhana, Karṇa, Śakuni have to pay for their sins", he roared.

Ironically, Arjuna tried pacifying Krishna. "Vāsudeva! Wars, defeat, victory, deceit are a part of kṣatrīya's life," he said. But these arguments did not satisfy Śrī Kṛṣṇa. He was filled with remorse. He was certain that he would have never allowed the debacle to happen, had he been there in the assembly.

"Indulging in gambling, intoxication and womanising, are the evils that destroy a human being. Man loses everything he has, wealth and self-respect. What is left at the end of the game are ill feelings and words that start as a friendly banter but end in enmity. I would have reasoned with them to not gamble but if they had refused to listen to me, I would have used force to defeat Duryodhana and his equally evil friends and allies," Kṛṣṇa said.

**Lessons from the Bhagavad Gītā 16.21**

The verse from Bhagavad Gītā 16.21 states:

tri-vidham narakasyedam dvāram nāśanam ātmanaḥ
kāmaḥ krodhas tathā lobhas tasmād etat trayam tyajet

Three gates lead to hell – lust, anger, and greed. These destroy the self. Therefore, one should abandon these three.

How it aligns with the Mahābhārata

The three qualities – kāma (lust), krodha (anger), and lobha (greed) – play significant roles in the actions and downfall of Duryodhana:

- Kāma: Kāma is a driving force behind many pivotal events in the Mahābhārata.

    o Duryodhana's lust for power leads him to act unjustly, initiating the Kurukṣetra war.

    o Karna's lust for power makes him support Duryodhana in all his wrongdoings and brings shame and conflict to him and his allies.

- Krodha:

    o Duryodhana's anger at his perceived humiliation at Indraprastha drives him to extract revenge through the game of dice.

    o Aśvatthāmā's anger (as we will see later) after his father's death leads him to commit heinous acts, like releasing the Brahmāstra against the unborn Pāṇḍava heir.

- Lobha:

  o Duryodhana's greed for the Pāṇḍava kingdom drives the gambling match and subsequent exile of the Pāṇḍavas.

  o Śakuni's manipulative greed for the reflected power that he would achieve if his nephews, the Kauravas, became the rulers, further fuels the discord.

The Mahābhārata demonstrates how unchecked lust, anger, and greed cause suffering and destruction, reinforcing the importance of renouncing these qualities to uphold dharma.

How it aligns with Kṛṣṇa-bhakti

In bhakti, the rejection of these qualities is essential for spiritual progress. The philosophy emphasizes surrender to Lord Kṛṣṇa and cultivating pure devotion (bhakti) free from material contaminations like lust, anger, and greed.

- Kāma: Bhakti teaches that lust is a perverted reflection of pure love for Kṛṣṇa. True fulfilment comes from transforming material desires into spiritual love (prema) directed toward the Lord.

- Krodha: Devotees are encouraged to practice titikṣā (forbearance) and channel anger constructively. For instance, anger can be used in service to the Lord, such as protecting dharma or defending devotees, as exemplified by Hanumān or Bhīma in righteous contexts.

- Lobha: Instead of material greed, devotees are encouraged to develop a spiritual greed (laulyam) for Kṛṣṇa's mercy and association. This positive transformation aligns the individual's desires with divine will.

Both the Mahābhārata and bhakti highlight the destructive nature of lust, anger, and greed and advocate their renunciation. In the Mahābhārata, renouncing these vices is shown as essential for maintaining societal dharma, while their rejection is a prerequisite for progressing on the path of bhakti. Both ultimately lead individuals toward a life of harmony, self-realization, and connection with the Supreme.

Three Gates to Self-Destruction

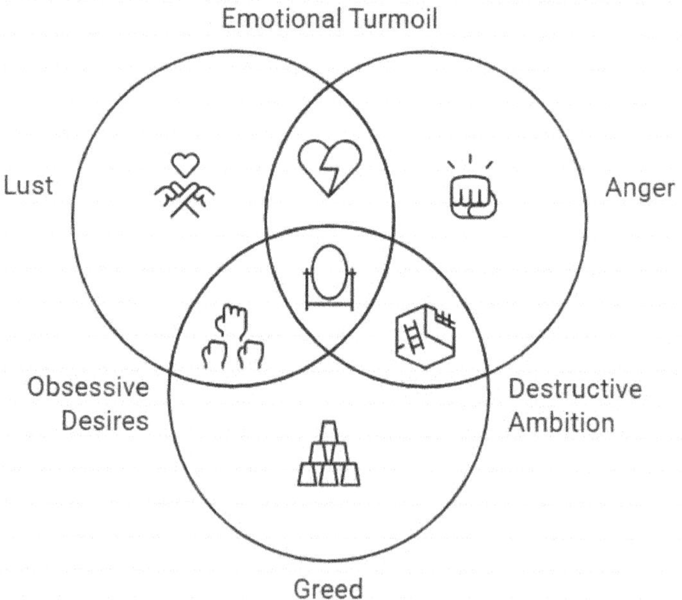

17. Arjuna's quest for divine weapons

One day, Vyāsadeva visited the Pāṇḍavas in exile and said, "After these thirteen years, you will face a fierce war with the Kauravas. You will be victorious, but to prepare for the battle, Arjuna, you must seek divine weapons during your exile."

Arjuna replied, "I will follow your advice, sire."

Vyāsa instructed, "Go to Mount Kailāśa and worship Lord Śiva. He will give you what you need."

Arjuna travelled to Mount Kailāśa and meditated on Lord Śiva. After a long period, Lord Śiva, disguised as a hunter, appeared with his wife Pārvatī and his followers in the form of female hunters. A wild boar attacked Arjuna, and both he and the hunter shot arrows at it, killing it. Arjuna, upset that someone else had shot his prey, challenged the hunter.

Arjuna said, "Who are you to take what is mine?"

The hunter (Lord Śiva) responded, "I shot it first. Prove you are the better archer."

The contest between Arjuna and the hunter escalated into a fierce exchange of arrows, each trying to prove their superiority. When neither could gain the upper hand, they engaged in hand-to-hand combat. To Arjuna's surprise, the hunter showed no signs of fatigue, while he himself began to tire. Acknowledging his limits, Arjuna requested a brief respite, and the hunter, with unexpected grace, agreed.

Seizing the moment, Arjuna fashioned a clay Śiva liṅga and earnestly prayed to Lord Śiva for strength. As a mark of his devotion, he placed a garland on the liṅga. When he turned back toward the hunter, he was astonished to see the same garland now adorning the hunter's neck. The realization struck him like lightning – the hunter was none other than Lord Śiva in disguise. Overwhelmed with reverence, Arjuna immediately fell at Lord Śiva's feet, seeking his blessings.

Arjuna said, "My Lord, forgive me for not recognizing you."

Lord Śiva, pleased by Arjuna's devotion, said, "Ask for a boon."

Arjuna requested the Paśupata weapon, and Śiva granted it, saying, "Use it wisely in the war ahead."

After Lord Śiva departed, other devas appeared, offering Arjuna their divine weapons.

Indra, Arjuna's father, invited him to Indraloka. Arjuna rode a golden chariot to Indra's palace, where he was honoured. He learned music and dance from Citrasena, the chief of the Gandharvas. There, Arjuna met the apsara, Urvaśī.

Urvaśī, enchanted by Arjuna, wanted him to be her lover. However, Arjuna respectfully declined saying, "Mother Urvaśī, I cannot. I see you as my mother."

Urvaśī, hurt by his rejection, cursed him, "In your final year of exile, you will become a eunuch among women."

Arjuna said, "I accept your curse, but may it serve a greater purpose."

Urvaśī, softened by Arjuna's self-control, blessed him saying, "This curse will protect you in your last year of exile, helping you remain hidden from your enemies."

Thus, Arjuna continued his journey, now armed with divine weapons and a deeper understanding of his destiny in the coming war.

Lessons to be learned

- Preparation and determination – Success requires dedication, preparation, and patience. Arjuna's willingness to endure challenges during his exile reflects the importance of persistence in achieving goals.

- Reverence and devotion – Arjuna's devotion to Lord Śiva demonstrates that humility and reverence for higher powers bring blessings and strength.

- Self-control and respect – Arjuna's respectful response to Urvaśī's proposal shows the value of adhering to one's principles and treating others with dignity, even in difficult situations.

- Accepting consequences gracefully – Arjuna's acceptance of Urvaśī's curse with humility shows that setbacks can be turned into advantages with the right mindset.

Values reflected

- Respect (ādara): Arjuna's reverence for sages, devas, and even his adversary (Lord Śiva disguised as a hunter); also Arjuna's reverence towards Ūrvaśī, who he considered a mother.

- Wisdom (viveka): Recognizing Lord Śiva's divine nature and using his curse for a strategic advantage.

- Patience (titikṣā): Arjuna's perseverance during long meditation and struggles.

- Humility (vinaya): Seeking forgiveness from Lord Śiva and bowing to the devas.

- Self-discipline (tapas): Arjuna's meditation and adherence to his principles, even under temptation.

- Truthfulness (satya): Remaining true to his values despite external pressures.

- Courage (dhairya): Facing challenges, including combat with Lord Śiva, and boldly embracing his destiny.

18. Duryodhana humbled

During Arjuna's stay in Indraloka, he received many powerful weapons from the devas. Indra gave Arjuna his powerful Vajra, teaching him how to use it. He then returned to his brothers. The Pāṇḍavas were thrilled to see him back, and

"Welcome back, Arjuna!" Yudhiṣṭhira said, his face lighting up with joy. "We've missed you."

"We are ready to fight for our kingdom, brother," Arjuna replied, happily holding up the weapons.

Meanwhile, in Hastināpura, Duryodhana was plotting again. He found out that the Pāṇḍavas were living as ascetics in the Dvaita forest and decided to use the opportunity to attack them. He thought, "If we start a quarrel, we can kill them all."

He said to Śakuni and Karṇa, "Let's go to Dvaitavana on the pretext of an annual stock-taking of the cows. We'll then challenge the Pāṇḍavas to a fight and end their exile."

When Duryodhana and his large army reached Dvaitavana, they split up, exploring in groups. Duryodhana went up to the Pāṇḍavas and began to boast about his opulent life and his luxuries. The Pāṇḍavas did not react.

Meanwhile, one group arrived at a pond near the Pāṇḍavas' hermitage and found Gandharvas bathing there.

"Clear out of the pond!" they ordered, puffing up with arrogance. "Make room for King Duryodhana to bathe!"

The Gandharvas ignored them, continuing to enjoy themselves. Furious, Duryodhana himself came to fight with them. "Leave now or face the consequences!" he shouted.

The Gandharva leader, Citrasena, stepped forward, unfazed. "We have no intention of obeying your orders," he replied calmly. Moments later, his arrows rained down, scattering Duryodhana's forces and leaving Duryodhana bound and captured.

The Kauravas, in desperation, sought the help of Yudhiṣṭhira. "Please, help us! Our prince has been captured. Only you have the power to save him."

Yudhiṣṭhira, after a moment's reflection, turned to Arjuna. "Arjuna, go to his aid," he said solemnly. "Duryodhana is still our family. Despite everything that has happened, we must show compassion. Though we may be at odds with him, to the world, we are all brothers – 105 in total."

As Arjuna faced Citrasena in battle, he suddenly paused, recognizing him. "Citrasena!" Arjuna called out. "You are our friend, not our enemy."

Pleased to see his friend Arjuna, Citrasena released Duryodhana, who was now humbled and defeated. With his pride shattered, Duryodhana returned to Hastināpura, his spirit crushed by the realization of his own folly.

Lessons from the Bhagavad Gītā 17.15

The verse from Bhagavad Gītā 17.15 fits the incident of Duryodhana's capture by the Gandharvas. The verse states:

anudvega-karaṁ vākyaṁ satyaṁ priya-hitaṁ ca yat

svādhyāyābhyasanaṁ caiva vāṅ-mayaṁ tapa ucyate

Austerity of speech consists in speaking words that are truthful, pleasing, beneficial, and not agitating to others, and also in regularly reciting Vedic literature.

BG 17.15 and the incident of Duryodhana's capture

Bhagavad Gītā 17.15 describes verbal austerity (vāṅ-mayaṁ tapa) as speech that can pass through five filters. Speech should be:

- non-agitating (anudvega-karaṁ),

- truthful (satyaṁ),

- pleasing (priyam),

- beneficial (hitaṁ),

- cultivated and enriched by scriptural wisdom (svādhyāyābhyasanaṁ).

Duryodhana and his followers' arrogance and aggressive speech led to his defeat and capture. Therefore, his followers sought Yudhiṣṭhira's help. Yudhiṣṭhira's measured and compassionate response directing Arjuna to rescue Duryodhana despite Duryodhana having used his words to try and incite a fight with the Pāṇḍavas exemplifies anudvega-karaṁ vākyaṁ. His words upheld truth and conveyed a higher sense of dharma: the duty to protect one's kin, even in the face of hostility. This act of verbal and practical dharma demonstrated priya-hitaṁ (beneficial and pleasing speech), as it fostered unity and set an example of moral conduct.

In contrast, Duryodhana's speech throughout the event – arrogant and confrontational with the Gandharvas – lacked the qualities of vān-mayaṁ tapa. His words provoked conflict and brought about his downfall, showing the destructive consequences of unrestrained speech.

Relevance in Kṛṣṇa-bhakti

In bhakti, speech is seen as an expression of a devotee's inner state and devotion. Words are meant to glorify the Lord, inspire others toward bhakti, and reflect spiritual wisdom. The qualities of vān-mayaṁ tapa are central to bhakti teachings:

- Non-agitating speech (anudvega-karam): Devotees avoid harsh or divisive words, focusing instead on nurturing harmony and devotion. The principle of ahimsa in thought, word, and deed aligns with using speech that avoids causing distress to others. Even when addressing faults, devotees are taught to speak with compassion and humility.

- Truthfulness (satyam): Devotees are encouraged to speak in ways that glorify Kṛṣṇa and disseminate His teachings. Truth in bhakti transcends mundane facts, aiming to illuminate spiritual realities.

- Pleasing and beneficial speech (priya-hitam): Devotees focus on speech that inspires and uplifts others, fostering devotion and love for Kṛṣṇa. This is particularly evident in the lives of saints like Śrī Caitanya Mahāprabhu and Śrīla Prabhupāda, who used speech to guide others toward bhakti.

- Scriptural foundation (svādhyāyābhyasanam): The

emphasis on studying scriptures ensures that speech is rooted in eternal truths and serves a higher purpose.

In bhakti, speech is a tool for spiritual elevation, integral to devotional practices like chanting the holy names of the Lord (nāma-saṅkīrtana) and discussing the scriptures (kathā). Controlled and purposeful speech aligns with the path of bhakti. Devotees apply this by prioritizing words that are saturated with divine purpose, avoiding gossip or unnecessary criticism, and ensuring that speech contributes to the collective spiritual progress of society.

By embodying these principles, devotees transform speech into an offering to Kṛṣṇa, making it an act of devotion.

Refining Speech through Five Filters

Back in Hastināpura, Dhṛtarāṣṭra and Bhīṣma spoke to Duryodhana. "You must make peace with the Pāṇḍavas," Bhīṣma urged. "Share the kingdom with them."

But Duryodhana refused. "I will never share the kingdom with them. This is my right!"

The Pāṇḍavas continued their exile in Dvaitavana. One day, Yama, the god of death, appeared before Yudhiṣṭhira, testing his commitment to truth.

"You've been loyal and just, Yudhiṣṭhira," Yama said. "I want to grant you a boon. Ask for anything."

Yudhiṣṭhira thought for a moment. "Please, protect us for the thirteenth year of our exile. We need to remain undetected."

Yama nodded. "It's done. Go to King Virāṭa's kingdom for the thirteenth year. There, you will remain hidden."

The Pāṇḍavas, now ready to leave, travelled to Virāṭa's kingdom, where they would spend the next year in disguise.

Lessons to be learned

- Pride comes before a fall – Duryodhana, despite his arrogance and refusal to share the kingdom with the Pāṇḍavas, was humbled when he was captured by the Gandharvas. His defeat and subsequent return to Hastināpura serve as a lesson that pride and arrogance can lead to downfall. True strength lies in humility.

- Mercy in the face of adversity – The Pāṇḍavas, despite the animosity between them and Duryodhana, still agreed to help him when he was captured by the Gandharvas. This act of mercy shows the importance of forgiveness and the bond of family, even in times of conflict.

- True courage is in recognizing peace – Arjuna demonstrated great courage not only in battle but also in recognizing his allies among the Gandharvas and refraining from further violence once he identified Citrasena. His willingness to act and make peace reflects true bravery.

- The power of truth in difficult times – Yudhiṣṭhira's commitment to truth is highlighted when he seeks Yama's blessing to protect the Pāṇḍavas during their final year of exile. His unwavering adherence to truth, even in times of hardship, teaches us the value of righteousness.

Values reflected:

- Humility (vinaya): Duryodhana's capture and his eventual humbling.

- Forgiveness (kṣamā): The Pāṇḍavas' decision to help Duryodhana, despite his past wrongs.

- Courage (dhairya): Arjuna's courage in both battle and peace.

- Truthfulness (satya): Yudhiṣṭhira's dedication to truth and righteousness.

19. The Pāṇḍavas in disguise

The thirteenth year was upon them and the Pāṇḍavas were determined to remain incognito. They hid their weapons in a tree in the cremation grounds where no one went and entered Virāṭa's kingdom, where they were not recognized. King Virāṭa welcomed them and offered them work.

Yudhiṣṭhira, disguised as the brāhmaṇa, Kaṅka, became a game entertainer and dice player for the king. Bhīma became Vallabha, a cook. Arjuna, cursed by Urvaśī to remain a eunuch for a year, became Bṛhannalā, teaching music and dance to the princess, Uttarā. Nakula became Granthika, a horse trainer, and Sahadeva became Tantipāla, a cattle herder. Draupadī became Sairandhrī, a maid to Queen Sudeśnā.

Things were going well until Kīcaka, the queen's brother and commander of Virāṭa's army, became interested in Draupadī. One day, he approached her.

"Draupadī, I want to marry you," Kīcaka demanded.

Draupadī, shocked, replied, "I am already married and have five powerful divine husbands. I cannot marry you."

Kīcaka, feeling insulted, decided to force himself into her room that night. Draupadī was terrified and ran to Bhīma. "Please, save me, Bhīma. He is planning to enter my room tonight."

Bhīma, ever the protector, disguised himself as Draupadī and lay in wait. When Kīcaka entered, Bhīma sprang up and struck him down before he could react.

The next morning, the queen found Kīcaka's lifeless body in Draupadī's room. She was confused. "Draupadī, what happened?"

"I don't know who killed him," Draupadī said. "He entered my room without permission, and when I screamed, someone came and killed him."

The queen apologized for her brother's actions but never discovered the truth.

Meanwhile, Duryodhana sent spies to find the Pāṇḍavas. When he heard about Kīcaka's death, he suspected Bhīma. "Who else could have killed Kīcaka? No ordinary man could do that," he thought. "I suspect it was Bhīma."

Determined to find the Pāṇḍavas, Duryodhana sent his army to Virāṭa. He planned to attack the kingdom and force the Pāṇḍavas into exile again.

20. The Battle with Duryodhana's Army

As Duryodhana's army approached Virāṭa, Yudhiṣṭhira offered the Pāṇḍavas' services to King Virāṭa. "We owe you our ·safety, my lord," Yudhiṣṭhira said. "Allow us to help you in this time of danger."

Virāṭa agreed, and all the Pāṇḍavas, except Arjuna, joined the army. They quickly captured Suśarma, a general of Duryodhana.

But Duryodhana, Karṇa and the Kurus attacked Virāṭa's palace from the opposite direction. The only person left to defend the palace was the young prince, Uttara. He claimed he couldn't go to war because he didn't have a charioteer.

Arjuna, overhearing this, stepped forward. "I'll be your charioteer," he said. "Let me help you."

Uttara was reluctant, but Arjuna reassured him. "I'll drive the chariot, and you can fight. Together, we'll win."

Arjuna blew his conch, and Duryodhana's army immediately recognized him. Duryodhana, thinking the Pāṇḍavas were still in exile, was shocked when he learned their thirteenth year had ended. Arjuna fought bravely and single-handedly defeated Duryodhana's army. Duryodhana fled the battlefield in defeat.

After the battle, Yudhiṣṭhira spoke to King Virāṭa. "We've been in exile under your protection for the past year. We are grateful for your help."

Virāṭa was pleased to see the Pāṇḍavas. "You are always welcome in my kingdom. I would like to give my daughter, Uttara, in marriage to your son, Abhimanyu."

The Pāṇḍavas agreed, and soon, a grand wedding was held for Abhimanyu and Uttarā, uniting the families.

21. War declared

After the wedding, Kṛṣṇa advised Virāṭa and Drupada to go to Dhṛtarāṣṭra and ask for the Pāṇḍavas' kingdom back. Sanjaya was sent to deliver the message. Dhṛtarāṣṭra called a meeting with the elders, but Duryodhana refused to give up even a tiniest part of the kingdom.

"I will not share the kingdom with the Pāṇḍavas," Duryodhana declared. "The only way they'll get it back is through war."

The elders were troubled, and Kṛṣṇa went to Duryodhana, hoping to convince him to avoid war. But Duryodhana remained stubborn.

"Kṛṣṇa," Duryodhana said coldly, "You're too biased towards the Pāṇḍavas. If they want their kingdom back, they will have to fight for it." Duryodhana then tried to capture and imprison Kṛṣṇa, the messenger, which was against all principles of dharma. At this time, Kṛṣṇa revealed his universal form, the viśva-rūpa which could be seen by a few of the pious Kurus.

Kṛṣṇa then left Hastināpura and told Yudhiṣṭhira and Kuntī that peace was no longer an option. War was inevitable.

Kuntī, fearing for her sons, went to Karṇa, who was performing his morning rituals. She revealed a shocking truth to him.

"Karṇa, you are my son with the sun-god, Sūrya," she said. "You were born to me before I married Pāṇḍu. I had to abandon you, but you were raised by a charioteer."

Karṇa was stunned. "So, I am one of the Pāṇḍavas?"

"Yes," Kuntī replied. "Please, Karṇa, don't fight against your brothers who are on the side of dharma. Join them instead."

Karṇa's eyes welled up with tears as he looked at his mother. "Mother, I promise I will spare all of them… except Arjuna. I must fight him to avenge the public insult he caused me. In the end, you will still have five sons – either Arjuna or me, but not both."

Kuntī said, "I bless you, Karṇa, but I fear for you. War is coming, and no one knows what the future holds."

Karṇa nodded solemnly. "I will fight until the end."

With a heavy heart, Kuntī left, knowing that the war was drawing near, and her sons would soon face their fate.

Lessons to be learned

- The dangers of stubbornness – Duryodhana's refusal to share the kingdom with the Pāṇḍavas, even after Kṛṣṇa's intervention and his rejection of the wise counsel of elders, shows the destructive power of stubbornness and pride. His unwillingness to seek peace led to inevitable conflict, which could have been avoided with humility and open-mindedness. His actions show that unchecked pride can lead to significant loss and suffering.

- The power of compassion and family bonds – Despite all the wrongs Karṇa has done, Kuntī, a mother, pleads with Karṇa to join his brothers, urging him to forsake his loyalty to Duryodhana and fight for dharma. Her love and compassion for her son transcended the enmity between the families. Karṇa's response to his mother shows that family bonds are powerful, but duty can sometimes overshadow even familial ties.

- The perils of loyalty to the wrong cause – Karṇa's loyalty to Duryodhana, despite knowing that Duryodhana's actions are driven by envy and malice, illustrates the dangers of misplaced loyalty. His unwavering support for Duryodhana, even when it conflicts with his higher moral duty, leads him down a path of destruction. Loyalty is a powerful force, but it must be directed towards righteous causes and not blind loyalty to individuals who promote unethical actions.

- The consequences of ignoring dharma – Despite his inner conflict, Karṇa's loyalty to Duryodhana prevents him from fully embracing his dharma. His refusal to join his brothers, who stand for justice, is a tragic example of how ignoring one's true duty can lead to grave consequences. One's duty (dharma) must take precedence over loyalty to any individual or cause that contradicts it. Ignoring dharma leads to destruction, both for oneself and others.

- The cost of blind loyalty – Karṇa's blind loyalty to Duryodhana costs him his relationships with his brothers and his own sense of identity. His inability to reconcile his loyalty to Duryodhana with the truth of his heritage prevents him from making a choice that might have led to peace and redemption.

- The truth can be painful – Kuntī's revelation to Karṇa about his true heritage was an emotional moment. She knew the implications of her revelation and feared for all her sons' safety. Karṇa's acceptance of this truth and his decision to fight to the death illustrates the complex relationship between duty, honour, and family. Sometimes, the truth is painful, but it is necessary for growth and understanding. Sacrifice is often required when choosing a higher purpose, even if it means personal loss.

Values reflected

- Compassion (dayā / karuṇā): Kuntī's compassion for her son Karṇa is evident as she seeks to protect him and urges him to join the Pāṇḍavas, despite the inevitable conflict between the families. Her actions reflect the deep love and care she has for her children.

- Truthfulness (satya): The truth about Karṇa's heritage, revealed by Kuntī, brings a significant moment of realization and change in the story. Despite the pain it causes, the truth is necessary to resolve Karṇa's inner conflict and his understanding of his identity.

22. Śrī Kṛṣṇa speaks the Bhagavad Gītā

The great battle of Kurukṣetra was about to begin. The Kauravas and the Pāṇḍavas were gathering their forces. Draupadī's brother, Dhṛṣṭadyumna, a fearless warrior, was chosen to lead the Pāṇḍava army, while the Kauravas had the mighty Bhīṣma, a warrior like no other, as their commander. But Bhīṣma, despite his immense strength, was bound by duty to fight for the Kauravas, even though he knew this war was unjust.

As Duryodhana approached Bhīṣma to formally take command, Bhīṣma laid down two conditions. "I will not personally harm the Pāṇḍavas," he said firmly. "I will only fight their soldiers. And secondly, Karṇa must not be allowed to fight while I am the commander."

Meanwhile, Kṛṣṇa found himself in a difficult position. Both the Pāṇḍavas and the Kauravas were his cousins. So, when both Arjuna and Duryodhana came to him seeking his help, Kṛṣṇa offered them a choice. "I can either lend you my powerful army or I can join you as an individual," he said. Arjuna, ever wise, chose Kṛṣṇa, valuing his counsel above even an entire army. Duryodhana, on the other hand, happily accepted Kṛṣṇa's army.

The day of battle arrived, and the vast Kurukshetra plain became the site of a war unlike any before. The Kaurava army was much larger, but the Pāṇḍavas had Kṛṣṇa's guidance. As the battle began, Arjuna, stationed in his chariot with Kṛṣṇa as his charioteer, looked across the battlefield. Seeing his beloved family and teachers on the opposite side, a deep sorrow gripped his heart. He couldn't bring himself to fight.

Kṛṣṇa, seeing Arjuna's distress, spoke smilingly, "Arjuna, your duty as a warrior is to fight for what is righteous. These men you see before you are souls, bound by their karma. It is not you who decides their fate, but the greater plan of the universe. Fight, Arjuna, for justice and truth." Kṛṣṇa went on to speak the Bhagavad Gītā, guiding Arjuna through the principles of dharma (duty) and selfless action. He explained karma yoga, the path of action performed without attachment to results, as a means to purifying the mind and to liberation.

Kṛṣṇa then elaborated on bhakti yoga (devotion) as the means to reach him and jñāna yoga (knowledge) as a path to attain self-realization and connect with the Supreme. He emphasized the impermanence of the material body and the immortality of the soul, encouraging detachment from worldly concerns. He explained the modes of nature, sattva (goodness), rajas (passion), and tamas (ignorance), and their influence on human behaviour. At Arjuna's request Kṛṣṇa revealed his universal form, the viśvarūpa, showing his divine omnipotence, and also his four-armed form.

Finally, Kṛṣṇa told Arjuna, "Do you have any questions or doubts that you need me to clarify? If not, Arjuna, think deeply about the various methods of reaching me (yoga) that I have spoken about and then do as you wish7."

Enlightened by the words of the Bhagavad Gītā, Arjuna was inspired and resolved to fulfil his duty. He took up his bow once again and prepared to fight.

Lessons from the Bhagavad Gītā 2.47 and 9.27

Śrī Kṛṣṇa provides Arjuna with timeless instructions that guide not only his immediate decision but also the spiritual and moral framework for all humanity. Two verses, 2.47 and 9.27, highlight distinct but interconnected aspects of this guidance, emphasizing duty (karma) and devotion (bhakti).

Bhagavad Gītā 2.47

---

7 *iti te jñānam ākhyātaṁ guhyād guhya-taraṁ mayā vimṛśyaitad aśeṣeṇa yathecchasi tathā kuru: Thus I have explained to you knowledge more secret than all secrets. Deliberate on this deeply, and then do as you wish. (BG 18.63)*

karmaṇy evādhikāras te mā phaleṣu kadācana
mā karma-phala-hetur bhūr mā te saṅgo 'stv akarmaṇi

You have a right to perform your prescribed duty, but you are not entitled to the fruits of action. Never consider yourself the cause of the results of your activities and never be attached to not doing your duty.

Bhagavad Gītā 9.27

yat karoṣi yad aśnāsi yaj juhoṣi dadāsi yat
yat tapasyasi kaunteya tat kuruṣva mad-arpaṇam

Always think of Me, become My devotee, worship Me and offer your homage unto Me. Thus, you will come to Me without fail. I promise you this because you are very dear to me.

How these verses align with the Mahābhārata

Verse 2.47 explains the principle of niṣkāma-karma – performing one's duty without attachment to the fruits of actions. Arjuna is paralyzed by doubts, questioning whether fighting in the war leading to potential destruction of his kin, aligns with dharma.

Śrī Kṛṣṇa advises Arjuna to focus on his duty as a kṣatriya, urging him to act without attachment to the potential outcomes. By dedicating himself to his responsibilities and serving as an instrument of the Lord's divine instructions, Arjuna can rise above selfish motives and align his actions with dharma. This principle resonates throughout the Mahābhārata, where figures like Bhīṣma and Vidura embody unwavering commitment to duty without seeking personal gain.

Kṛṣṇa's guidance introduces the profound philosophy of karma-yoga, emphasizing action performed with full dedication while remaining detached from its fruits. Through verse 9.27 Kṛṣṇa encourages Arjuna to view his duty as an offering to the Supreme, free from selfish desires or the fear of failure. Faced with the moral complexities of battle, Arjuna is exhorted to rise above his personal emotions and act in harmony with dharma, the universal principle of righteousness. Through this, Kṛṣṇa reveals a path of selfless service, empowering Arjuna to act with clarity, purpose, and divine alignment.

Relevance in Kṛṣṇa-bhakti

This message aligns closely with the practice of bhakti-yoga, or devotional service to Kṛṣṇa. The philosophy emphasizes surrendering one's actions and results to the Supreme Lord without selfish desires.

Key connections include:

1. Devotion without expectation:

Bhakti teaches that all actions should be performed as an offering to Kṛṣṇa, without expecting personal rewards. This principle mirrors the idea of detachment from the fruits of actions outlined in BG 2.47. For example, devotees chant the holy names or serve others without seeking material gains, focusing instead on pleasing the Lord.

2. Detachment from material results:

Just as Arjuna is encouraged to fight without attachment to victory or defeat, a bhakta (devotee) engages in the world without attachment to material successes or failures. Instead, their focus is on their daily duties which are performed as an offering to Kṛṣṇa leading to their developing a deeper relationship with the Lord.

3. Avoiding inaction:

The verse also warns against avoiding one's duty (mā te saṅgo 'stv akarmaṇi). For example, the duty of a student is to study, that of a householder is to earn a living to provide for the family, and so on. Similarly, devotees are encouraged to remain active in service to Kṛṣṇa along with their worldly duties, whether through temple worship, kīrtana, or Kṛṣṇa kathā, rather than withdrawing from the world out of fear of imperfection.

4. Surrender to Kṛṣṇa's will:

As per the Bhagavad Gītā and Kṛṣṇa-bhakti, the ultimate goal is surrender to Kṛṣṇa's will. By relinquishing the desire for personal gain and acting as an instrument of divine will, a devotee transcends karma and achieves a very loving relationship with Kṛṣṇa throughout their lives.

In both the Mahābhārata and Kṛṣṇa-bhakti, BG 2.47 and 9.27 serve as guiding principles for a life of selfless action, detachment, and surrender to higher purposes. They underscore that true success lies in aligning all one's actions with dharma and devotion to the Supreme.

BG 2.47 and modern psychology

This verse highlights the importance of focusing on one's duty (or Dharma) without being attached to the results or immediate outcomes of those actions. The concept here is selfless action or karma-yoga, which is performing one's duties without the expectation of rewards, but with the understanding that righteous actions lead to a more meaningful life and ultimate happiness.

In modern psychology, the concept of **Flow** aligns with this verse. Flow is a psychological state where a person is fully immersed in an activity, experiencing deep focus, enjoyment, and a sense of effortlessness. In this state, time seems to slow down or speed up, and the person is completely present in the task.

For details about the concept of Flow and how it can be applied to the lives of young people, see **Appendix 3.**

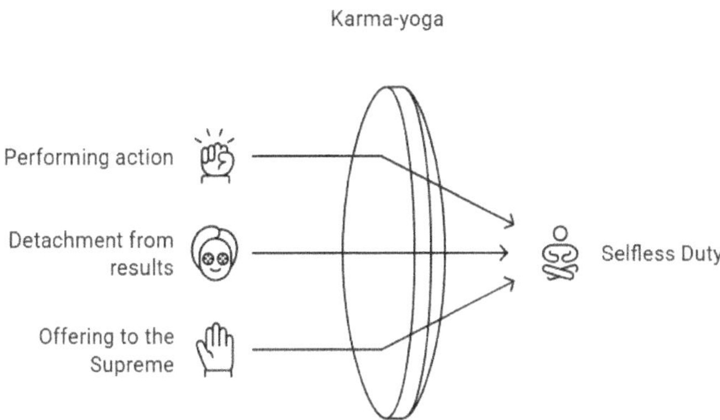

23. The war rages on

The battle was fierce, and Bhīṣma led the Kaurava forces with great strength, slaying thousands of soldiers. Despite their best efforts, the Pāṇḍavas were losing ground.

That night, Yudhiṣṭhira, the eldest Pāṇḍava, called a council to discuss their strategy. The next day, they managed to slow Bhīṣma's progress, but the war was far from over.

The battle continued for days. Duryodhana grew impatient with Bhīṣma, taunting him for not being able to win the war quickly. Bhīṣma, though a hero, admitted that the Pāṇḍavas were blessed with divine powers. He promised Duryodhana that the war would end soon, or he would leave the battlefield.

On the evening of the ninth day, the Pāṇḍavas approached Bhīṣma. "Please tell us how we can defeat you," they requested. Bhīṣma looked affectionately at them. "Know that I will never shoot arrows at a woman, or one that was a woman before or one bearing a feminine name, or one whose form resembles a woman's. I will, therefore, not slay Śikhaṇḍī. Arjuna, keep Śikhaṇḍī's chariot in front and shoot arrows at me from behind. Thus, you will defeat me." Accordingly, the Pāṇḍavas attacked Bhīṣma the next day. The great Bhīṣma fell, pierced by arrows, and the day of battle ceased to honour him.

As Bhīṣma lay dying on a bed of arrows, he asked Arjuna to raise his head. Arjuna did so by shooting an arrow into the ground under his head. Then, when Bhīṣma asked for water, Arjuna shot another arrow into the earth, and water poured forth. Even Karṇa came to honour Bhīṣma, seeking his blessings.

Bhīṣma said he would die only when the sun returned to the northern hemisphere.

The war raged on. Duryodhana chose Droṇācārya as the next commander, but Droṇa, despite his power, was not as effective. Droṇācārya vowed to capture Yudhiṣṭhira, and in the heat of battle, he killed Drupada, the father of Dhṛṣṭadyumna, the commander of the Pāṇḍavas. This act sparked a deep vow for revenge from Dhṛṣṭadyumna.

Soon, Droṇācārya decided to use the wheel formation, the "cakra-vyūha8," to trap Yudhiṣṭhira. Arjuna was the only one who knew how to break it, but he was occupied at the other side of the battlefield. Abhimanyu, Arjuna's son, came to Yudhiṣṭhira's support. "I can break into the cakra-vyūha but I do not know how to escape, he said.

"Don't worry about that. You go in and I'll follow immediately after and together we can break out," Yudhiṣṭhira assured Abhimanyu. Abhimanyu fought his way into the cakra-vyūha and was trapped inside the formation. Yudhiṣṭhira was stopped by Jayadratha who prevented him from going after Abhimanyu. Seeing Abhimanyu trapped, the Kaurava warriors closed in on him and breaking all the rules of warfare, attacked him together from all sides, even when he was on foot and unarmed. They mercilessly slayed him, and the entire Pāṇḍava camp was plunged in grief.

---

8 Also known as Padmavyūha, this is a multi-tiered defensive formation that looks like a blooming lotus (padma) or disc (cakra) when viewed from above. As per this military strategy, a specific stationary object or a moving object or person could be captured, surrounded and fully secured during battle.

Arjuna, upon learning of his son's death, broke down. He vowed to kill Jayadratha, the man who had sealed Abhimanyu's fate. The next day, Jayadratha tried to hide within the Kaurava formation, but Kṛṣṇa used his divine owers to create an illusion, making it appear as though the sun had set. With the Kaurava forces relaxed, Arjuna took the opportunity and killed Jayadratha.

Despite the death of Jayadratha, the war continued with relentless fury. Droṇācārya vowed to kill one of the Pāṇḍavas the next day. Kṛṣṇa, knew of Drona's secret promise to lay down his arms if his son, Aśvatthāmā, died. He therefore devised a plan. Kṛṣṇa approached Yudhiṣṭhira and advised him, "Yudhiṣṭhira, announce that Aśvatthāmā is dead. It is necessary to win this war." Yudhiṣṭhira, renowned for his unwavering commitment to truth, faced a moral dilemma. Reluctantly, he stepped forward and declared, " Aśvatthāmā is dead," pausing briefly before adding softly, "the elephant." Drona, consumed by grief at hearing the first part of the statement and failing to hear the clarification, let his weapons fall. Seizing the moment, Dhṛṣṭadyumna struck, killing Droṇa.

Karṇa then took over as the Kaurava commander. His skills were unmatched, and the Pāṇḍavas began losing ground. But then Bhīma called upon his son, Ghaṭotkaca, who fought fiercely, causing panic in the Kaurava camp. In the end, Karṇa was forced to use the Śakti weapon, given to him by Indra, to kill Ghaṭotkaca. This was a huge blow for Karṇa who had been saving the weapon to kill Arjuna.

As the war continued, Arjuna faced Karṇa in a final, intense battle. Karṇa, unarmed and vulnerable, pleaded with Arjuna to stop while his chariot wheel was fixed. Kṛṣṇa, however, argued that Karṇa had not followed the rules of the war when killing Abhimanyu and urged Arjuna to strike. Karṇa was killed. The Kaurava forces, now without their greatest warrior, began to falter.

On the eighteenth day of the war, Duryodhana was found hiding in a pond, unwilling to face his defeat. Bhīma challenged him to a duel, and though the fight was intense, Bhīma, following Kṛṣṇa's advice, struck Duryodhana below the belt, breaking his thigh as a punishment for his insults to Draupadī.

With Duryodhana's death, the Kaurava army collapsed. The great war, born of Duryodhana's unchecked arrogance and consuming envy, which claimed the lives of hundreds of thousands, had at last reached its tragic conclusion.

Lessons from the Bhagavad Gītā 16.4

The verse from Bhagavad Gītā 16.4 describes traits belonging to individuals of a demoniac (āsurī) nature:

dambho darpo 'bhimānaś ca krodhaḥ pāruṣyam eva ca

ajñānaṁ cābhijātasya pārtha sampadam āsurīm

"Hypocrisy, arrogance, conceit, anger, harshness, and ignorance are the qualities of those born with demoniac nature, O Pārtha."

BG 16.4 as a Character Study of Duryodhana

The verse BG 16.4 describes the qualities of individuals with demoniac tendencies, including hypocrisy (dambhaḥ), arrogance (darpaḥ), conceit (abhimānaḥ), anger (krodhaḥ), harshness (pāruṣyam), and ignorance (ajñānam). These traits align closely with Duryodhana's character in the Mahābhārata.

Definitions applied to Duryodhana:

- Dambhaḥ (hypocrisy):

Dambhaḥ refers to religious ostentation and pretending to be virtuous. Duryodhana often pretended to act in the interest of dharma while concealing his malicious intentions, such as inviting the Pāṇḍavas to the house of lac under the guise of goodwill.

- Darpaḥ (arrogance):

Darpaḥ is described as pride arising from wealth, relations, or status. Duryodhana's arrogance stemmed from his royal lineage and position as the eldest son of Dhṛtarāṣṭra. This arrogance led him to constantly slight others, including Vidura and even Lord Kṛṣṇa.

- Abhimānaḥ (excessive haughtiness):

Abhimānaḥ (stated as atimānaḥ in some versions) relates to

overestimating one's respectability. Duryodhana's excessive pride in his position made him unwilling to accept counsel, even when it was in his best interest, such as Vidura's and Bhīṣma's advice to avoid war.

- Krodhaḥ (anger):

Krodhaḥ is described as a mental state akin to "heart-burning" that harms oneself and others. Duryodhana's anger, especially toward the Pāṇḍavas, consumed him and drove his decisions, including declaring war, which ultimately led to the destruction of the Kuru dynasty.

- Pāruṣyam (harshness):

Pāruṣyam refers to rudeness and the habit of speaking harshly. Duryodhana displayed harshness in his treatment of Draupadī during the dice game and in his cruel words to the Pāṇḍavas throughout the Mahābhārata.

- Ajñānam (ignorance):

Ajñānam denotes a lack of discrimination about what should or should not be done. Duryodhana's inability to discern right from wrong, despite being repeatedly warned, reflects his deep ignorance. His obsession with power blinded him to the catastrophic consequences of his actions.

Relevance to Kṛṣṇa-bhakti

The traits described in BG 16.4 represent obstacles to devotional life and spiritual progress. They highlight the qualities that must be avoided by those aspiring to cultivate pure bhakti. Here's how this teaching integrates with the principles of bhakti:

- Opposition to dambha (hypocrisy):

Hypocrisy is a major impediment in devotional service. Bhakti emphasizes saralata (simplicity) and ananya-bhakti (undivided devotion), which require genuine humility and honesty.

- Darpa (arrogance) and abhimāna (haughtiness):

Pride and overestimation of oneself are contrary to the spirit of trinād api sunīcena (being humbler than a blade of grass), as stated by Śrī Caitanya Mahāprabhu. True devotees attribute all success to Kṛṣṇa's mercy, not their own achievements.

- Freedom from krodha (anger):

Anger disrupts the peace of mind needed for chanting and meditation. Devotees are encouraged to practice titikṣā (forbearance) and view difficulties as opportunities to depend on Kṛṣṇa.

- Rejection of pāruṣyam (harshness):

Harshness is antithetical to the compassionate dealings of a devotee. The teachings of Lord Caitanya inspire followers to cultivate dayā (compassion) and karuṇā toward all living beings.

- Overcoming ajñānam (ignorance):

Ignorance of one's spiritual identity is the root of material entanglement. By studying scripture like the Gītā and engaging in nāma-saṅkīrtana (chanting Kṛṣṇa's names), devotees dispel ignorance and develop viveka (discrimination between eternal and temporary).

This verse fits within bhakti's broader framework of self-purification and character building. It serves as a reminder to devotees to examine their own tendencies and strive to uproot demoniac traits through the 3S:

- Sādhu-saṅga (association with devotees): To imbibe daivī qualities.

- Śravaṇa and kīrtana (hearing and chanting): To cleanse the heart of impurities.

- Sevā (service) to Kṛṣṇa: The ultimate means to transcend ego, anger, and ignorance, fostering pure love (prema) for the Lord.

Lessons from Duryodhana's character

Duryodhana's life serves as a cautionary tale. By identifying and avoiding the āsurī qualities he embodied, practitioners can cultivate divine virtues (daivī sampad), which are essential for both spiritual growth and harmonious relationships. For devotees, this reinforces the path of humility, self-discipline, and unconditional surrender to Lord Kṛṣṇa. By contrasting Duryodhana's nature with Kṛṣṇa's teachings, this verse reinforces the necessity of aligning one's life with divine virtues for spiritual progress and harmony.

Path to Pure Love

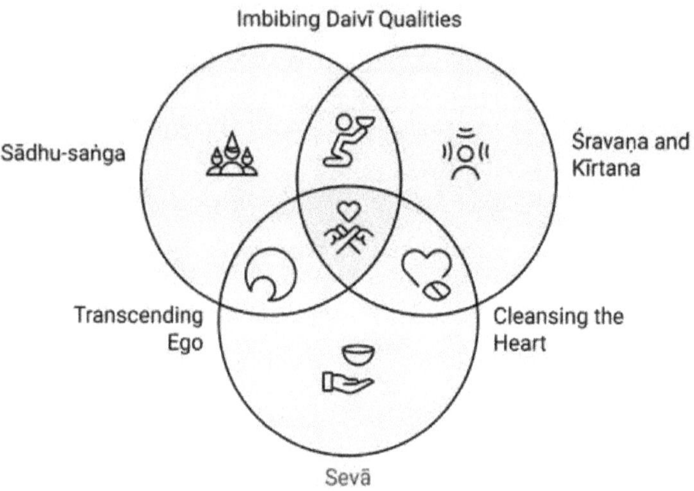

24. Draupadī's sons killed

The Pāṇḍavas returned to their camp, victorious, though deeply saddened by the immense loss. That night, Aśvatthāmā, in a fit of rage and vengeance for his father Droṇa's death, secretly entered the Pāṇḍavas' camp and killed their sleeping sons. The next morning, Draupadī discovered the horrific crime and overcome with grief, demanded justice. Arjuna, deeply angered by the loss of his nephews, vowed to avenge their deaths and bring Aśvatthāmā to her. He set out to capture him, with Kṛṣṇa by his side, both determined to make the murderer face the consequences of his actions. Aśvatthāmā, realizing the enormity of his crime, fled to Sage Vyāsa's hermitage, but Arjuna pursued him.

A fierce confrontation ensued, and in desperation, Aśvatthāmā invoked the powerful Brahmāstra weapon, threatening destruction. Arjuna, equally prepared, readied his own Brahmāstra to counter the attack. At this moment, Sage Vyāsa intervened, urging them to withdraw their weapons to avoid annihilation. As Arjuna complied, Aśvatthāmā, unable to retract his weapon, diverted it towards Uttarā, who was pregnant with Parīkṣit, the last hope of the Pāṇḍava lineage. Kṛṣṇa intervened, protecting the unborn child and ensuring his survival.

Draupadī, even though heart-broken over the murder of her innocent young sons, asked that Aśvatthāmā be punished but not killed. "I can understand the pain Aśvatthāmā's mother, Kṛpī, would feel if she found out that her only son was killed," she said. "I am going through such tribulation now and cannot allow that to happen to anyone, least of all to the wife of our guru, Droṇācārya."

As punishment, Aśvatthāmā was cursed by Kṛṣṇa to wander the earth in shame, suffering for the rest of his life for his heinous act.

Lessons to be learned

- The consequences of greed and arrogance – Duryodhana's refusal to share the kingdom, driven by greed and arrogance, led to the destruction of the Kauravas and untold suffering. His actions illustrate that selfishness and pride bring about personal and collective ruin.

- The power of divine wisdom – Kṛṣṇa's teachings in the Bhagavad Gītā transformed Arjuna from a state of despair into one of clarity and resolve. This shows how divine wisdom and guidance can illuminate the path of righteousness even in the most challenging circumstances.

- The impermanence of material power – Kṛṣṇa's teachings on the soul's immortality and the fleeting nature of material success remind us that worldly power is temporary, while spiritual growth and realization endure.

- The strength of selflessness and duty – Arjuna's willingness to put aside his personal attachments and fulfil his duty as a warrior, along with Yudhiṣṭhira's unwavering commitment to truth and dharma, demonstrate the strength of selflessness in upholding justice and moral principles.

- Forgiveness and empathy amidst tragedy – Despite the horrific murder of their sons by Aśvatthāmā, the Pāṇḍavas chose not to execute him. Their decision highlights the power of forgiveness as a higher path, rising above vengeance and placing trust in divine justice.

- Compassion in leadership – Kṛṣṇa's role as a guide, mediator, and protector, even for those who opposed him, showcases the importance of compassion in leadership. True leaders act with empathy, seeking justice while minimizing harm.

- Patience in adversity – The Pāṇḍavas faced immense challenges throughout the 18-day war. Their ability to remain steadfast, adapt to losses, and continue their efforts highlights the importance of patience in overcoming hardships.

- Courage in the face of adversity – Whether it was Abhimanyu's fearless stand in the cakra-vyūha, Bhīma's determination to defeat Duryodhana, or Arjuna's resolve to face Bhīṣma and Karṇa, the war is a testament to the courage required to uphold righteousness in the face of overwhelming challenges.

- Gratitude for divine intervention – The Pāṇḍavas continually acknowledged Kṛṣṇa's divine intervention as the cornerstone of their survival and success. This reflects the importance of gratitude in recognizing the support and blessings one receives.

Values reflected

- Humility (vinaya): The fall of Duryodhana serves as a lesson in humility. His arrogance and inability to compromise led to his downfall, teaching us the importance of remaining grounded and respectful.

- Wisdom (viveka): Kṛṣṇa's teachings provided Arjuna with clarity, helping him overcome his moral confusion. This reflects the value of wisdom in making righteous decisions during difficult times.

- Self-discipline (tapas): The Pāṇḍavas displayed immense self-discipline by prioritizing their duties over personal desires, maintaining focus throughout the prolonged war.

- Forgiveness (kṣamā): The Pāṇḍavas' decision to spare Aśvatthāmā, despite their grief, exemplifies the power of forgiveness in rising above personal revenge and maintaining dharma.

- Compassion (dayā / karuṇā): Kṛṣṇa's actions, from guiding Arjuna to protecting Uttarā's unborn child, illustrate the deep compassion that is essential in leadership and justice.

- Patience (titikṣā): The Pāṇḍavas endured immense suffering, showing that patience is crucial in achieving long-term goals and overcoming obstacles.

- Truthfulness (satya): Yudhiṣṭhira's adherence to truth, even when it conflicted with his personal emotions, underscores the importance of honesty in upholding dharma.

- Courage (dhairya): The bravery displayed by Abhimanyu, Bhīma, and Arjuna in fulfilling their responsibilities, despite overwhelming odds, highlights the necessity of courage in pursuing righteousness.

- Gratitude (kṛtajñatā): The Pāṇḍavas' acknowledgment of Kṛṣṇa's role in their lives reflects the value of gratitude for divine guidance and support in times of need.

25. After the war

The dust was beginning to settle after the great war, but the Pāṇḍavas still had one important task to complete. With heavy hearts, they set off for Hastināpura to meet King Dhṛtarāṣṭra, the blind father of their fallen enemies. Kṛṣṇa, ever the guide and friend, travelled with them, alongside Vidura, to offer comfort to Dhṛtarāṣṭra and Gāndhārī.

"King Dhṛtarāṣṭra," Kṛṣṇa began, his voice soft but firm, "the war was inevitable. It has brought sorrow to everyone. Both the Pāṇḍavas and the Kauravas have suffered great losses. Now is the time to heal. Accept Yudhiṣṭhira as your son and bless the Pāṇḍavas to rule with wisdom."

Dhṛtarāṣṭra's eyes filled with tears, and he broke down, seeking solace in his brother Vidura's arms. Yudhiṣṭhira, ever respectful, bowed deeply and touched the feet of Dhṛtarāṣṭra and Gāndhārī. With a blessing, Dhṛtarāṣṭra finally accepted Yudhiṣṭhira as the rightful king of Hastināpura.

However, Gāndhārī's grief ran deep, and she could not forgive Kṛṣṇa. Through her tears, she spoke, her voice trembling with anger. "You are the root of all this destruction, Kṛṣṇa. You could have prevented this, but you didn't. May your family face the same fate as the Kauravas and be wiped out from the earth!"

Kṛṣṇa didn't try to stop her, for he understood the inevitability of what was to come.

The group then travelled to where Bhīṣma lay, still waiting for the moment of his death. There, Bhīṣma, his spirit strong even in his final moments, blessed the Pāṇḍavas, and taught them various lessons on dharma and how to rule the kingdom wisely. He also spoke the Viṣṇu-sahasra-nāma, the thousand names of Viṣṇu. Finally, fixing his eyes and mind on the form of Śrī Kṛṣṇa in standing in front of him, he gave up his glorious life.

Yudhiṣṭhira still felt immense guilt at the death of millions of men killed in the war. Sage Vyāsadeva advised him to perform the Aśvamedha yajña to bring him peace of mind.

As the years passed, Dhṛtarāṣṭra, Gāndhārī, Kuntī, and Vidura withdrew to the forest to meditate and attain liberation. A forest fire consumed them all, and Sanjaya, their caretaker, was the sole survivor. He returned to the Pāṇḍavas with the heartbreaking news.

Uttarā, the wife Abhimanyu, gave birth to Parīkṣit. Parīkṣit was the only heir left, having survived the deadly assault by Aśvatthāmā when he was still in his mother's womb.

Eventually, Gāndhārī's curse on Kṛṣṇa began to take its toll. The Yādavas, Kṛṣṇa's clan, began to fight among themselves. Even Kṛṣṇa and his brother Balarāma left this earth, and with no successors, their kingdom fell into disarray.

When the Pāṇḍavas heard of the Yādavas' destruction and Kṛṣṇa's passing, they knew the time had come to retire from the world. They decided to crown Parīkṣit as the new ruler and leave the world behind. They discarded their weapons into the river and began their final journey to the Himālayas, seeking peace in the mountains. To their surprise, a dog began following them, keeping pace with the Pāṇḍavas.

As they climbed, the journey grew harder, and one by one, Draupadī and the four Pāṇḍava brothers died, succumbing to the harsh conditions of the climb. Only Yudhiṣṭhira and the dog remained as they reached the summit of the Himalayas.

At the peak, Lord Indra appeared in his chariot, waiting to take Yudhiṣṭhira to heaven. "Come, Yudhiṣṭhira," Indra called. "Your righteousness has earned you a place in the heavens."

Yudhiṣṭhira, looking down at the dog who had loyally followed them, turned to Indra. "I will not go without the dog," he said firmly.

Indra was taken aback. "A dog to heaven? Why would you bring a dog?"

Yudhiṣṭhira replied, "This dog has followed us all this way. I cannot abandon it now. If it cannot go with me then I too refuse to go to heaven."

At that moment, the dog transformed into Yama, the god of death, in his true form. "I have been testing your commitment to justice, Yudhiṣṭhira," he said with a smile. "Your faith and adherence to dharma has never wavered. You shall be rewarded."

Together, Yudhiṣṭhira and the dog ascended to svarga, where he was reunited with his family.

And thus ends the epic story of the Mahābhārata. The lessons of duty, righteousness, and sacrifice live on forever, as future generations continue to draw strength from its wisdom.

Lessons to be learned

Lessons to be learned

- Grieving together leads to healing – The Pāṇḍavas' respectful interaction with Dhṛtarāṣṭra and Gāndhārī demonstrated that humility and empathy can help mend relationships, even after great loss.

- Understanding the inevitability of time – Kṛṣṇa's actions reflected the teaching that one must embrace duty and consequences without resentment.

- Faith and righteousness are always rewarded – Yudhiṣṭhira's loyalty to the dog revealed his steadfast righteousness, emphasizing that staying true to one's values leads to ultimate rewards.

- Sacrifice is central to duty – The Pāṇḍavas relinquished their worldly attachments during their final journey, highlighting that sacrifice is often necessary to fulfil one's spiritual purpose.

- The cycle of life and death is universal – The destruction of the Yādavas, and the departure of the Pāṇḍavas demonstrate the impermanence of life and the eternal nature of dharma.

Values reflected

- Respect (ādara): The Pāṇḍavas honoured Dhṛtarāṣṭra and Gāndhārī despite their enmity, showing deep reverence for elders and relationships.

- Wisdom (viveka): Kṛṣṇa's teachings and Yudhiṣṭhira's adherence to righteousness reflected sound judgment and understanding of dharma.

- Compassion (dayā / karuṇā): Yudhiṣṭhira's refusal to abandon the dog revealed his empathy and care for all living beings.

- Humility (vinaya): The Pāṇḍavas' behaviour after the war illustrated their modesty and lack of arrogance despite their victory.

- Self-discipline (tapas): The Pāṇḍavas' renunciation of their kingdom and journey to the Himalayas highlighted their ability to ignore their desires and focus on higher goals.

- Truthfulness (satya): Yudhiṣṭhira's unwavering honesty

and commitment to his values throughout the epic demonstrated the importance of truth in every action.

- Courage (dhairya): The Pāṇḍavas faced the challenges of war, loss, and renunciation with bravery and strength.

Appendix 1

Delayed gratification and the Marshmallow Experiment

Delayed gratification, or deferred gratification, is the ability to resist the temptation of an immediate reward in favour of a more valuable and long-lasting reward later. It involves forgoing a smaller, immediate pleasure to achieve a larger or more enduring benefit in the future.

There are two paths we can take in any given situation: one is the path of avoiding pain in the moment, and the other is the more difficult path of delaying pleasure for a bigger purpose. The behaviour of most people is ruled by the "pleasure principle," a term coined by Sigmund Freud, the Austrian neurologist and the founder of psychoanalysis. The pleasure principle is the instinctual seeking of pleasure and avoidance of pain in order to satisfy biological and psychological needs.

This is contracted with the concept of the "reality principle," which explains the ability to delay gratification when a situation doesn't call for immediate gratification. Whether it's working part-time and saving money for college, mastering a skill like playing an instrument, avoiding peer pressure and choosing healthy options, delayed gratification can yield tremendous returns while helping to develop a tolerance for waiting.

The Stanford Marshmallow Experiment

The Stanford Marshmallow Experiment is a psychological study that tested delayed gratification in children. It demonstrated that those who could endure initial discomfort (waiting for a larger reward later rather than taking a smaller immediate reward) tended to achieve greater success in life.

The experiment, conducted by psychologist Walter Mischel and his colleagues in the late 1960s and early 1970s, is a landmark study in understanding self-control and delayed gratification. The experiment involved children aged four to six, who were presented with a marshmallow and given a choice: they could eat the marshmallow immediately or wait for 15 minutes without eating it and receive a second marshmallow as a reward.

Mischel and his team observed that some children could wait while others gave in to immediate temptation. Follow-up studies over decades revealed significant correlations between the ability to delay gratification and various measures of success later in life. Those who waited for the second marshmallow tended to have higher academic achievements, better health, and more stable relationships as adults.

The study demonstrated that self-control and the ability to delay gratification are critical traits for long-term success and well-being. It also highlighted that these abilities are not entirely innate; they can be influenced by environmental factors and learned over time. While the experiment has faced scrutiny and reinterpretation in recent years, its core message – that self-discipline plays a vital role in personal development – remains highly influential in psychology and education.

Here is the link to a video where Walter Zimbardo, a colleague of Mischel reprises the experiment:

https://www.youtube.com/watch?v=y7t-HxuI17Y

Examples of delayed gratification for young people

1. Academic and career goals:

    - Studying for exams: Choosing to study instead of hanging out with friends, knowing good grades will help secure college admissions.

    - Saving money for college: Working a part-time job and saving rather than spending on unnecessary items.

    - Mastering a skill: Practicing an instrument, sport, or coding diligently instead of giving up for immediate leisure.

2. Health and fitness:

    - Healthy eating choices: Opting for a nutritious meal instead of junk food to maintain energy and long-term health.

    - Exercising regularly: Staying consistent with workouts instead of lounging around, focusing on the long-term benefits of fitness.

3. Social and personal growth:

    - Avoiding peer pressure: Resisting the urge to join harmful activities to maintain integrity and avoid long-term consequences.

- Investing in friendships: Supporting a friend during tough times rather than seeking only immediate fun, building stronger relationships over time.

4. Financial discipline:

- Saving for a Big Purchase: Saving birthday money or part-time job earnings for something significant like a car or a laptop instead of spending impulsively.

5. Spiritual and emotional development:

- Practicing meditation or yoga: Spending time in meditation rather than scrolling through social media, aiming for mental clarity and peace.

- Reading uplifting literature: Choosing to read thought-provoking or spiritual books rather than watching mindless entertainment, focusing on personal growth.

Delayed gratification teaches patience, discipline, and a long-term perspective, helping young people build a solid foundation for future success and happiness.

Connection between BG 18.37 and the experiment

This concept of delayed gratification ties in closely with Bhagavad Gītā 18.37, which describes sāttvika happiness:

yat tad agre viṣam iva pariṇāme 'mṛtopamam
tat sukhaṁ sāttvikaṁ proktam ātma-buddhi-prasāda-jam

That happiness which seems like poison at first but is like nectar in the end – arising from the serenity of one's mind in self-realization – is said to be sāttvika.

1. Enduring the "Poison": In the experiment, the initial waiting period is analogous to the "poison" in the verse. It is challenging for children to resist immediate gratification, just as it is hard to endure the difficulties of self-discipline and effort in life.

2. Reaping the "Nectar": Those children who successfully waited for the larger reward align with the verse's message. The "nectar" they experienced parallels the long-term benefits of self-discipline, whether in terms of better academic performance, health, or career success, as shown in follow-up studies.

3. Sāttvika happiness as inner discipline: The verse emphasizes happiness arising from wisdom and self-control. Similarly, the experiment illustrates that enduring discomfort for a higher goal requires the self-awareness and inner discipline that the Gītā attributes to sāttvika qualities.

Both the verse and the experiment highlight the principle that true fulfilment often comes from enduring short-term challenges for long-term benefits. Whether through mastering one's impulses (as in the experiment) or practicing discipline in spiritual and material pursuits (as emphasized in the Gītā), the outcome is consistent: greater happiness, success, and inner satisfaction.

In contrast to verse 18.37, Bhagavad Gītā 18.38 states:

viṣayendriya-saṁyogād yat tad agre 'mṛtopamam
pariṇāme viṣam iva tat sukhaṁ rājasaṁ smṛtam

That happiness which arises from the contact of the senses with their objects, and which appears like nectar at first but poison in the end is declared to be of the nature of passion (rājasa).

The verse describes rājasa sukha – happiness that seems sweet initially but turns sour in the long run. This would contradict the behavior of children who failed the experiment by indulging in the immediate gratification of eating the first marshmallow.

The experiment provides empirical evidence for the benefits of resisting rājasa sukha (short-term pleasure) and aiming for sāttvika sukha (delayed, enduring happiness), thus highlighting the importance of self-control in achieving long-term benefits.

Appendix 2

Making the mind a friend

Managing the mind is essential for young people to achieve focus, success, and inner peace. Here are some practical methods based on spiritual teachings, including the Bhagavad Gītā, and modern strategies:

1. Mindfulness and Meditation

    - Practicing daily meditation, even for 10–15 minutes, helps calm the mind and improve focus. Focusing on breathing or chanting a mantra like the Hare Kṛṣṇa mahāmantra clears mental clutter.

    - BG 6.6: "For one who has conquered the mind, the mind is the best of friends; but for one who has failed to do so, his mind will remain the greatest enemy."

2. Regulating food and sleep

    - Eating sattvic (pure, healthy, and light) food enhances clarity of thought and energy. Avoid overeating or consuming excessive junk food.

    - Getting adequate sleep (7–8 hours) ensures a rested mind, reducing stress and irritability.

BG 6.17: "He who is regulated in eating, sleeping, working, and recreation can mitigate all material pains by practicing yoga."

3. Goal setting and time management

- Setting clear goals provides direction for the mind. Breaking tasks into smaller, achievable steps reduces overwhelm.

- Time-blocking and prioritizing tasks prevent procrastination and distraction. Staying productive keeps the mind engaged.

4. Physical exercise and Yoga

- Regular exercise, like walking, running, or yoga, releases endorphins, which stabilize the mind and emotions.

- Yoga āsanas (postures) and breathing exercises (prāṇāyāma) balance the body and mind, promoting self-discipline and control.

5. Limiting distractions

- Reducing screen time, especially on social media, curtails unnecessary thoughts and comparisons and helps to balance dopamine.

- Focusing on one task at a time (single-tasking) helps the mind develop discipline and deeper concentration.

6. Reading inspirational books

- Reading scriptures like the Bhagavad Gītā or motivational books strengthens resolve and provides guidance for self-control.

- Stories of personalities like Arjuna demonstrate how focus and determination can overcome any obstacle.

7. Association with positive influences

- Surrounding oneself with disciplined, focused, and virtuous people (like devotees or good friends) encourages positive habits.

- Bad association can lead to distractions and uncontrolled desires.

8. Chanting and devotional practices

- Chanting the Hare Kṛṣṇa mantra or engaging in kīrtana helps purify the mind and heart, fostering a connection with Kṛṣṇa.

- Regular prayer and devotional practices align the mind with spiritual goals, helping to overcome lower desires.

9. Self-reflection and journaling

- Taking time to reflect on one's thoughts and actions helps identify weaknesses and areas for improvement.

- Writing in a journal promotes clarity and allows young people to process their emotions constructively.

10. Practicing delayed gratification

- Young people can train their minds to resist instant pleasures in favour of long-term rewards. For instance:

- Studying now to secure good results later.

- Avoiding unhealthy snacks to maintain physical fitness.

11. Service and helping others

- Engaging in sevā (selfless service) fosters humility and reduces self-centred thoughts, redirecting the mind toward compassion and meaningful activities.

12. Daily routine and discipline

- Following a fixed daily routine (waking up early, performing morning prayers, studying, and exercising) instills discipline and minimizes idle time for distractions.

Young people can manage their minds through a combination of mindfulness, physical discipline, self-reflection, and spiritual practices. By following the teachings of the Bhagavad Gītā, like balancing work and rest (BG 6.17), associating with positive influences, and engaging in devotional service, they can gradually transform the mind into their greatest ally.

Appendix 3

The concept of Flow

Mihaly Csikszentmihalyi (pronounced me-hai chik-sent-me-ha-ee), a Hungarian-American psychologist, introduced the concept of Flow in his groundbreaking work on happiness and creativity.

Flow is a psychological state in which a person becomes fully immersed and engaged in an activity, experiencing intense focus, enjoyment, and fulfilment. It occurs when there is a perfect balance between the challenges of a task and the skills of the person performing it, leading to deep concentration and intrinsic motivation, and improved mental well-being.

Key Characteristics of Flow

- Complete concentration: The individual is fully focused on the task, with no room for distractions or external thoughts. Time often seems to either fly by or stretch indefinitely.

- Clear goals: There is a clear sense of what needs to be done, which guides the person's actions and decisions throughout the activity.

- Immediate feedback: The person receives instant feedback, whether through their own performance or external cues, which allows for continuous adjustment and improvement.

- Balance between challenge and skill: Flow occurs when the challenge of the activity is perfectly matched to the person's skill level. If the task is too easy, boredom sets in; if it's too difficult, frustration arises.

- Sense of control: In the Flow state, the individual feels a strong sense of control over their actions and the task at hand, without being overwhelmed or overly self-conscious.

- Loss of self-awareness: The person becomes so absorbed in the task that they lose awareness of themselves as separate from the activity. The experience is inherently rewarding and self-sustaining.

- Altered perception of time: During Flow, time often seems distorted – minutes can feel like hours, or hours can feel like minutes. This is because the mind is so absorbed in the activity that it loses track of time.

Examples of Flow

- In Sports: An athlete performing at their best, like a basketball player making precise shots during a game, might experience Flow.

- In Arts: A painter immersed in creating a painting or a musician lost in playing an instrument can enter a Flow state.

- In Work: A professional working on a challenging project or a coder writing a complex program may experience Flow when the task is both difficult and rewarding.

Benefits of Flow

1. Increased productivity

- Flow enhances performance and efficiency, as it encourages deep focus and full engagement.

2. Reduces anxiety and stress

- Focus on the present moment: Flow requires total focus on the task at hand, pulling attention away from worries about the past or future – key triggers for anxiety and stress.

- Activation of positive emotions: The engagement and sense of accomplishment experienced during Flow release endorphins and dopamine, which naturally counteract stress hormones.

3. Interrupts negative thought patterns

- When in a Flow state, the mind is fully occupied, leaving little room for repetitive negative thoughts often associated with depression or anxiety.

- Activities that induce Flow, such as creative work or physical exercise, serve as healthy escapes from ruminations.

4. Enhances learning, self-efficacy and confidence

- Flow helps individuals learn and improve skills quickly.

- Successfully engaging in and completing challenging tasks during Flow builds confidence. This boost in self-efficacy helps individuals feel more capable of handling life's difficulties.

5. Promotes emotional resilience

- Regular experiences of Flow contribute to emotional balance, helping individuals recover from setbacks more quickly.

- It creates a sense of control, even amidst external challenges, fostering a proactive mindset.

6. Strengthens mental clarity

- Flow aligns thoughts and actions, creating a harmonious state of mind. This clarity reduces cognitive clutter, making it easier to navigate overwhelming situations.

7. Offers purpose and meaning

- Engaging in activities that promote Flow – whether art, sports, music, or problem-solving – provides a sense of purpose and fulfilment, key components in combating feelings of emptiness or despair.

8. Improves sleep and physical health

- Since Flow reduces stress and promotes relaxation, it can contribute to better sleep patterns. Restful sleep is vital for mental health and resilience.

How to foster Flow for mental well-being

- Identify activities that are enjoyable and align with personal strengths.

- Create structured routines that incorporate Flow-inducing tasks.

- Practice mindfulness to improve focus and eliminate distractions.

While Flow is not a replacement for professional help in severe cases of mental illness, it can be a complementary tool. Incorporating Flow states into daily life can provide a reprieve from stressors and create a foundation for long-term mental well-being.

Flow and BG 2.47: The connection

1. Flow and detachment from results:

Csikszentmihalyi's concept of "flow" refers to a state where an individual is fully immersed in an activity with complete focus and enjoyment, without concern for external rewards or consequences. This resonates with BG 2.47, which emphasizes focusing on the process (one's duty) rather than being preoccupied with the outcome (results). In the flow state, the person is absorbed in the present task, mirroring Kṛṣṇa's advice to Arjuna about immersing oneself in duty with detachment from its results.

2.   Focus on the present moment:

The Gītā's teaching encourages one to live in the moment and give their best to the task at hand. Flow is also achieved when individuals focus on the activity they are performing without distractions. Both concepts highlight the importance of mindfulness and present-focused engagement without focus on the result.

3.   Optimal performance and dharma:

In the flow state, individuals often perform at their best because they are free from distractions such as fear of failure or excessive desire for success. Similarly, BG 2.47 advises detachment from the fruits of actions, allowing individuals to act effectively and in alignment with their dharma (duty) without the burden of stress or anxiety over the results.

4.   Joy in the process:

Mihaly explains that flow leads to intrinsic joy and fulfilment, not because of external rewards but because of the activity itself. This aligns with the Gītā's idea that true contentment comes from duty well performed, not from external gains.

Applying Flow to young lives

The concept of Flow can have a transformative impact on young people's lives. Flow refers to a state of complete immersion and focus in an activity, where one feels energized, fulfilled, and entirely present in the moment. This state is achieved when there is a perfect balance between the challenge of the task and the individual's skills.

1.   Finding the right activities:

Encourage young people to explore diverse interests, whether sports, music, art, or academics. Flow often occurs in activities they are passionate about, helping them discover joy in meaningful pursuits.

2.   Setting clear goals:

Young people can benefit from setting small, achievable goals within their tasks, whether completing a project, learning a skill, or improving performance. The idea here is to use clear goals to define the direction and structure of the task, making it easier to experience Flow.

3.   Eliminating distractions:

In today's fast-paced digital world, distractions are a major barrier to Flow. Teaching young people to create focused environments by turning off notifications, setting time blocks, or using techniques like the Pomodoro method can facilitate deeper concentration.

4.   Building skills gradually:

As Flow arises from the balance of challenge and skill, youth should be encouraged to step out of their comfort zones progressively. Mastery builds confidence and increases their capacity to handle more significant challenges.

5.   Intrinsic motivation:

Helping young people focus on the enjoyment of the process rather than external rewards (grades, trophies) fosters Flow. For example, rather than studying for marks, they can embrace learning as a way to grow intellectually.

6.   Mindfulness and presence:

Teaching mindfulness techniques such as meditation or breathing exercises can help young people become more present, reducing anxiety and fostering Flow.

Flow not only boosts performance and creativity but also enhances overall well-being by aligning actions with inner motivations. Integrating these principles can empower young individuals to approach life with enthusiasm, resilience, and a sense of fulfilment.

In modern life, the Gītā's teaching of working without attachment to results encourages individuals to focus on their tasks wholeheartedly. Similarly, cultivating the flow state can lead to personal and professional excellence, intrinsic motivation, and a deeper sense of satisfaction. Together, these ideas advocate for finding joy and fulfilment in meaningful work and living in harmony with one's purpose.

Application to Kṛṣṇa-bhakti

The concept of Flow can be meaningfully applied to Kṛṣṇa-bhakti.

1.   Focused devotion (Bhakti-yoga)

In Kṛṣṇa-bhakti, devotional service to Kṛṣṇa is central. When devotees practice bhakti with deep focus, whether through chanting the holy names (japa), singing kīrtanas, or engaging in other forms of service, they enter a state of Flow. This immersion in the act of worship and service allows them to transcend the material distractions and connect deeply with the divine, achieving a sense of peace, fulfilment, and joy.

Example: When a devotee is absorbed in chanting the Hare Kṛṣṇa mantra with full attention and devotion, they may experience the same qualities of Flow: deep concentration, joy, and a timeless connection with Kṛṣṇa.

2.   Balanced challenges in spiritual practice

In Flow, the challenge of the activity must be balanced with the individual's skill level. Similarly, in spiritual life, a practitioner's path should be suitably challenging yet manageable. The practice of sādhanā (spiritual disciplines) in bhakti, such as chanting, reading scriptures, and offering service, is designed to match the practitioner's spiritual capacity. This balance ensures engagement without overwhelming the devotee, encouraging steady spiritual progress.

Example: A devotee might begin by chanting a set number of mantras daily but gradually increase the number as they develop greater focus and commitment, experiencing deeper immersion in the process.

3.   Sense of purpose (Goal-oriented)

Flow is characterized by clear goals, which in bhakti align with the overarching aim of attaining pure love of God (prema). The devotee's focus on pleasing Lord Kṛṣṇa, cultivating humility, and performing their duties as an offering to Him provides them with clear spiritual goals. The practice of surrendering to Kṛṣṇa and recognizing Him as the ultimate goal keeps the devotee engaged, committed, and immersed in their spiritual journey.

Example: The goal of pleasing Kṛṣṇa through devotional service becomes a guiding principle for the devotee, similar to how a person practicing Flow has a clear goal that guides their actions.

4.   Loss of self-awareness (Ego transcendence)

In a state of Flow, the individual often loses self-awareness and becomes one with the task. In spiritual life, especially in bhakti, this loss of self-consciousness translates to ego transcendence. Through bhakti, the devotee forgets their material identity and becomes absorbed in Kṛṣṇa's service, experiencing a deep connection with the divine. This can be seen in how the devotees immerse themselves in their spiritual practices, losing their sense of the ego and focusing entirely on Kṛṣṇa.

Example: In the rāsa-līlā (the divine dance of Kṛṣṇa), the gopīs (milkmaids) experienced this state of Flow where their love and devotion to Kṛṣṇa transcended all material considerations. They enjoyed the rāsa-līlā for many hours without being fatigued, losing all sense of time and leading to pure spiritual bliss.

5.   Immediate feedback (Grace and guidance)

Flow is enhanced by the constant feedback loop that helps individuals adjust and improve. In bhakti, grace from Kṛṣṇa, spiritual guidance from a guru, and the support of the devotional community provide a form of immediate feedback. The devotee receives divine inspiration and the opportunity to learn from their experiences, which encourages continual growth in devotion.

Example: A devotee might receive a sense of spiritual satisfaction and direction when they are sincerely absorbed in devotional activities, reinforcing their commitment to the spiritual path.

6.   Enjoyment and bliss (Ānanda)

A central tenet of bhakti is ānanda or bliss, which arises from devotion to Kṛṣṇa. This concept aligns perfectly with the joy and fulfilment experienced in Flow. Devotees who are immersed in the service of Kṛṣṇa experience profound spiritual joy, especially when they perform acts of devotion with love and dedication. This bliss is not external but comes from a deep connection with the divine, much like the intrinsic enjoyment that Flow provides.

Example: A devotee engaged in kīrtana (devotional chanting) may feel the transcendental bliss that comes from the synchronized experience of singing the glories of Kṛṣṇa, similar to the joy felt in Flow.

Thus, the concept of Flow in psychology can be beautifully applied to bhakti. When devotees engage in their spiritual practices with full focus, balanced challenges, clear goals, and selflessness, they can experience a deep, rewarding connection with Kṛṣṇa, similar to the joy, fulfilment, and transcendence that Flow brings. Through this deep immersion in devotion, the devotee not only advances spiritually but also experiences the transformative power of pure love for God.

For more information:

https://positivepsychology.com/mihaly-csikszentmihalyi-father-of-flow/

Flow: The Psychology of Optimal Experience by Dr Mihaly Csikszentmihalyi PhD

https://www.researchgate.net/publication/224927532_Flow_The_Psychology_of_Optimal_Experience

Appendix 4

Guide to Sanskrit Pronunciation

Sanskrit is a highly refined, phonetic language. Therefore, accuracy in articulation and pronunciation is vitally important. Sanskrit is written exactly as it is spoken.

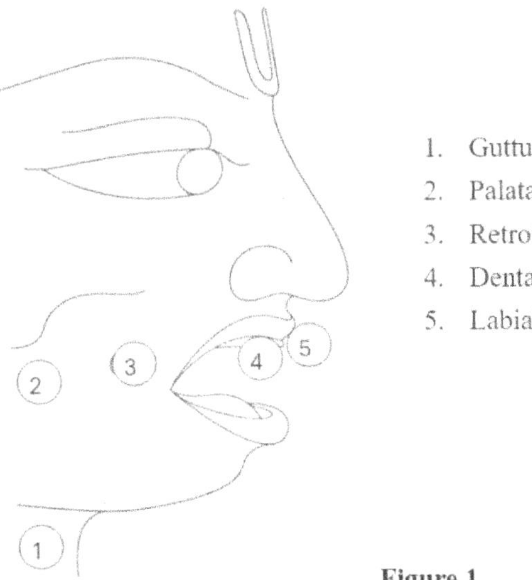

Figure 1

This guide uses IAST (International Alphabet of Sanskrit Transliteration) to help the user recognize the Sanskrit alphabet. It is based on Standard American English.

Figure 1 shows the various positions in the mouth where the tongue rests to produce the sounds of the alphabet.

Devanāgarī	IAST	Pronunciation guide
अ	a	Short, pure (single phoneme) vowel as in 'but'; constricted, with the mouth mostly closed.
आ	ā	Long (twice the duration of 'a'), pure vowel, as in 'far'; open, with the jaw dropped down.
इ	i	Short, pure vowel as in 'pit'. The mouth is wide.
ई	ī	Long (twice the length of 'i'), pure vowel as in 'meet'. The mouth is wider than 'i'.
उ	u	Short, pure vowel as in 'push' The lips are rounded.
ऊ	ū	Long (twice as long as 'u'), pure vowel as in 'pool'. The lips rounder than 'u'.
ऋ	ṛ	No English equivalent. Like the Italian flipped (or tongue-tip) 'r'. Note that this is a vowel.
ॠ	ṝ	No English equivalent. Like the

		Italian rolled 'rr'. Note that this is a vowel.
ळ	ḷ	As in 'clip'. Note that this is a vowel.
ए	e	As in 'they'. Diphthong-like phoneme (two vowels in one syllable); the point of articulation moves from the throat to the hard palate; narrow mouth.
ऐ	ai	As in 'aisle'. Diphthong-like phoneme where the point of articulation moves from the throat to hard palate; wide mouth.
ओ	o	As in 'go'. Diphthong-like phoneme where the point of articulation moves from the throat to the lips; rounded to more rounded lips.
औ	au	As in 'cow'. Diphthong-like phoneme where the point of articulation moves from the throat to the lips; wide to rounded lips.
◌ं	ṁ	Pure resonant nasal after a vowel, called anusvāra
◌ः	ḥ	Vowel aspiration called visarga; it takes the sound of the vowel preceding it.
क	ka	As in 'king'; unaspirated. This phoneme, and the next four, are all

			articulated at mouth position 1 – Guttural (see Figure 1 above).
ख	a	kh	As in 'workhorse. Heavily aspirated version of 'ka'.
ग		ga	As in 'go'; unaspirated.
घ	a	gh	As in 'dig-hard'; heavily aspirated version of 'ga'.
ङ		ṅa	As in 'sing'; a nasal consonant.
च		ca	As in 'chunk'; the tongue pressed flat against the hard palate; slightly aspirated. This phoneme, and the next four, are all articulated at mouth position 2 - Palatal (see Figure 1 above).
छ	a	ch	As in 'hitchhike; heavily aspirated version of 'ca'.
ज		ja	As in 'jar'; the tongue pressed flat against the hard palate; slightly aspirated.
झ		jha	As in 'hedgehog'; heavily aspirated version of 'ja'.
ञ		ña	As in 'canyon'; the tongue is pressed flat against the hard palate while saying 'n'; a nasal consonant.
ट		ṭa	As in 'top' except that the point of articulation is the tip of the tongue touching the dome of hard palate;

		unaspirated. This phoneme, and the next four, are all articulated at mouth position 3 - Cerebral (see Figure 1 above).
ठ	ṭha	As in 'rat-hole'; heavily aspirated version of 'ṭa'; the tip of the tongue touching the dome of hard palate.
ड	ḍa	As in 'dam' except that the point of articulation is the tip of the tongue touching the dome of the hard palate; unaspirated.
ढ	ḍha	As in 'red-hot'; heavily aspirated version of 'ḍa'; the tip of the tongue touching the dome of hard palate.
ण	ṇa	No English equivalent; similar to 'panda' except that the point of articulation is the tip of the tongue touching the dome of the hard palate; a liquid/nasal consonant.
त	ta	Similar to 'take' except that the tongue protrudes slightly between the bottom and top teeth; naspirated. This phoneme, and the next four, are all articulated at mouth position 4/dental (see Figure 1 above).
थ	tha	As in 'bath-house'; heavily aspirated version of 'ta'; the

			tongue protruding slightly between the bottom and top teeth.
द		da	Similar to 'them' except that the tongue is protruding slightly between the bottom and top teeth; unaspirated.
ध		dh a	Similar to 'withhold'; heavily aspirated version of 'da'; the tongue protruding slightly between the bottom and top teeth.
न		na	Similar to 'nit' except that the tongue is protruding slightly between the bottom and top teeth; a liquid/nasal consonant.
प		pa	Like 'pan'; unaspirated. This phoneme, plus the next four, are all articulated at mouth position 5 - labial (see Figure 1 above).
फ		ph a	As in 'up-hill'; heavily aspirated version of 'pa'.
ब		ba	Like 'bin'; unaspirated.
भ		bh a	As in 'clubhouse'; heavily aspirated version of 'ba'.
म		ma	As in 'miss'; a liquid/nasal consonant.
य		ya	As in 'yes'; Semi-vowel/approximant (a vowel-like consonant where the point of

			articulation changes depending on context).
र		ra	As in 'ray'; semi-vowel. Like the Italian rolled 'r' (will either be flipped or rolled depending on context). Note that this is a consonant.
ल		la	As in 'like'; semi-vowel; a consonant.
व		va	Semi-vowel; no English equivalent. More like a cross between a 'v' as in 'victory' and 'w' as in 'wellness'. The point of articulation starts at the lips and pulls back to the teeth.
श	*	śa	As in 'ship'; a sibilant; the tongue is very close to mouth position 2.
ष	*	ṣa	As in 'marshall'; a sibilant; the tongue is very close to mouth position 3.
स	*	sa	As in 'since'; a sibilant; the tongue very close to mouth position 4.
ह	**	ha	As in 'heavy'; a guttural; at mouth position 1. This phoneme is strongly aspirated.

Notes:

*These three sibilants require more breath and inner power to pronounce correctly. They are often part of conjunct consonants; two or more consonants not intermediated by a vowel. A sibilant at the beginning of a conjunct consonant will require even more strength applied to make the correct sound.

**This sibilant requires considerably more strength and movement of air to be pronounced correctly. This is also true for all the heavily aspirated consonants.

www.ingramcontent.com/pod-product-compliance
Lightning Source LLC
Chambersburg PA
CBHW041322120726
48005CB00014B/2092